Essential
Provence

by
ANNIE WILSON

Annie Wilson is an experienced
travel writer and researcher
who has produced guides to holiday
destinations throughout the world.

AA

Produced by AA Publishing

Written by Annie Wilson
Peace and Quiet section
by Paul Sterry
Series Adviser: Ingrid Morgan
Copy Editor: Christopher
Catling

Edited, designed and produced
by AA Publishing. Maps ©
The Automobile Association
1993

Distributed in the United
Kingdom by AA Publishing,
Fanum House, Basingstoke,
Hampshire, RG21 2EA.

The contents of this publication
are believed correct at the time
of printing. Nevertheless, the
publishers cannot accept
responsibility for errors or
omissions, nor for changes in
details given. Assessments of
attractions, hotels, restaurants
and so forth are based upon the
author's own experience and,
therefore, descriptions given in
this guide necessarily contain
an element of subjective
opinion which may not reflect
the publisher's opinion or
dictate a reader's own
experience on another
occasion.
**We have tried to ensure
accuracy in this guide, but
things do change and we
would be grateful if readers
would advise us of any
inaccuracies they may
encounter.**

A CIP catalogue record for this
book is available from the
British Library.

ISBN 0 7495 0519 2

Published by the Automobile
Association.

This book was produced using
QuarkXPress™, Aldus
Freehand™, and Microsoft
Word on Apple Macintosh™
computers.

Colour separation: by BTB
Colour Reproduction Ltd,
Whitchurch, Hampshire

Printed by: Printers Trento
S.R.L., Italy

*Front cover picture: Vaucluse
countryside*

Contents

INTRODUCTION	5	CULTURE, ENTERTAINMENT AND NIGHTLIFE	102
BACKGROUND	9	WEATHER AND WHEN TO GO	103
WHAT TO SEE	19	HOW TO BE A LOCAL	105
WEST VAUCLUSE	20	CHILDREN	105
LUBERON	37	TIGHT BUDGET	106
THE PLATEAU DE VAUCLUSE	41	SPECIAL EVENTS	107
NORTH VAUCLUSE	45	SPORT	109
WEST BOUCHES-DU-RHONE	49	DIRECTORY	111
THE CAMARGUE	64	LANGUAGE	125
EAST AND CENTRAL BOUCHES-DU-RHONE	68	INDEX	126
VAR AND ALPES-DE-HAUTE-PROVENCE	81		
PEACE AND QUIET Wildlife and Countryside in Provence	87		
FOOD AND DRINK	95		
SHOPPING	100		
ACCOMMODATION	101		

This book employs a simple rating system to help choose which places to visit:

 'top ten'

 ◆◆◆ do not miss
◆◆ see if you can
◆ worth seeing if you have time

Introduction and Background

INTRODUCTION

The dazzling delights of Provence, a land of wine and honey located in sunny southeastern France, have long been a magnet to visitors. The region's romantic landscapes and passionate people are as seductive as the embrace of the warm Provençal sunshine. If you are looking for a peaceful haven, for rustic simplicity, for a feast of historical sites and cultural activities, or if you want to splash out in truly sophisticated style, you can take your pick in Provence.

The strategic value of the area, bounded by the Mediterranean and the great Rhône river, has also been recognised by colonists, invaders and immigrants throughout the ages. The result is an impressively rich historical and cultural legacy, which is closely woven into the colourful fabric of Provençal life today.

An astonishing number of ancient buildings have survived, despite the turbulence of the region's past. Provence boasts the best-preserved Roman monuments in France – those in the old town of Arles, for example, the former capital of late Roman Gaul. These splendid monuments still play an active role in Provençal life and are used to stage a variety of cultural events.

Just as striking and more numerous are the monuments of the Middle Ages. One of the most magnificent is the Palais des Papes (Palace of the Popes) in the sophisticated walled city of Avignon, which owes much to the

The Grand Canyon du Verdon

Herbs from the hills

fact that the head of the Christian Church ruled from here during the 14th century. Fine abbeys, churches and castles dating from the Middle Ages are to be found all around Provence, but the most vivid link between the present and the medieval past lies in the region's countless picturesque hilltop villages and the old quarters of so many towns. Almost all remain as living communities, rather than historic showcases, and it is a joy to find so many that have survived intact.

The refined and stylish town of Aix-en-Provence has shined as a cultural centre since the Middle Ages, but here it is the glorious 17th and 18th-century architecture that has such eminently elegant appeal. On the coast, nearby, is the down-to-earth and chaotically cosmopolitan port of Marseille – the second-largest city in France, originally founded by the ancient Greeks. Like so many of the region's towns, Marseille has a choice of museums to arouse a deeper appreciation of this fascinating area.

The scenic variety offered by Provence is as rich as its history. Amid the heady Alpine heights of the northeast you will see spectacular panoramas looking over the rugged peaks, where local people live by herding sheep and goats in remote mountain

Scented sage

pastures. In the southwest, the peaks give way to the sweeping flat horizons and long sandy beaches of the Rhône delta and the marshy Camargue, home to wild horses and bulls, cowboys and gypsies and a wealth of birdlife, including flamingos.

In Provence, you will also find rocky hillsides scented with pine, wild rosemary and thyme, rolling slopes covered in a sea of vines or a fragrant haze of lavender, groves of ancient olives with their twisted trunks and shimmering silvery leaves, wild wooded plateaux cut by grand gorges and fertile valleys where crops, such as melons or sunflowers, grow in fields divided by ink-green cypress trees. All is bathed in a brilliant light, bringing these diverse landscapes into flattering focus and intensifying their colours.

It is this characteristic luminosity, and the profuse palette of natural hues, that has inspired so many artists. It is no coincidence that the countryside sometimes seems reminiscent of a painting: the area around Aix features in Cézanne's most celebrated works and Arles inspired Van Gogh to produce his best masterpieces. This region has long been a hotbed of creative endeavour and many places have a wealth of artistic associations. In summer, Provence bubbles over with cultural events of all sorts, especially at the major festivals.

The Provençal people are proud of their local traditions, which are as deep-rooted as the olive trees and the vines – and, in this extensively rural region, often connected with their profound love of the land. This applies especially to many of the colourful *fêtes* which take place through the year. The soul of Provence shines through in its unique folklore, costumes, legends, language and literature.

As a visitor you will undoubtedly be seduced by the sensual charms of Provence – the charismatic colours, the clear light and the heady scents. You can also enjoy its more cerebral pleasures and, of course, there is ample food for the body as well as for the mind and soul; the flavours of Provençal food and wine seem to reflect the sunshine – golden olive oil, bright red tomatoes, heady garlic,

INTRODUCTION

Cézanne's beloved Montagne Ste-Victoire

fragrant herbs and robust, fruity red wines. Provence is an area you can visit time and time again; its ability to interest and delight is as eternal as its azure skies, and in one short holiday you can only hope to taste a *soupçon* of the riches it has to offer. Travelling around and exploring provides endless treats, but you will need a car – unless you are adventurous and energetic enough to go by bicycle, on horse or on foot. Alternatively you could choose a peaceful and pretty spot where you can just sit and soak up the wonderful atmosphere along with the sun – falling into the relaxed rhythm of rural Provençal life, lingering over a *pastis* at a café shaded by plane trees and watching the locals play *boules*. Whether the antiquity, art or natural beauty of Provence appeals most to you, it is easy to be enchanted by the magic of this fascinating region.

BACKGROUND

Definitions of Provence can vary, depending on whether the region is seen in historical, popular or political terms. In Roman times, for example, *Provincia Romana*, from which Provence derived its name, covered most of southern France. The official administrative area of Provence today is made up of five *départements* – Vaucluse, Bouches-du-Rhône, Var, Alpes-de-Haute-Provence and Hautes-Alpes. This book is largely concerned with the first two *départements*, which together encompass the heart of 'old' Provence, lying close to the Rhône and including within their boundaries the majority of interesting sights. The book does not cover the French Riviera (Côte d'Azur) or the Alpes-Maritimes, which are sometimes linked to Provence for the purposes of tourist promotion (for this region see the AA guide *Essential French Riviera*).

Mellow wood and stone

Geography

Provence covers an area of almost 100 miles (160km) from east to west and is about the same distance north to south. In broad terms the landscape, climate and flora of this region is essentially Mediterranean but it is marked by great diversity.

Most places in Provence have a backdrop of hills, mountains or abrupt outcrops of rocky crags – apart from the Rhône delta. Fertile valleys lie beside the main rivers; most notable are the alluvial plains of the Rhône. This river has long been the lifeblood of Provence, playing a vital role in transport and trade from ancient times until very recently. It remains a major area for agriculture, and a variety of industry is also located on its banks.

The Durance is another important artery running from east to west through the centre of Provence – it flows into the Rhône just south of Avignon. To the north of this river, covering much of west Vaucluse, is the rich, intensively cultivated plain of the Comtat Venaissin. South of the Durance lie the plains of La Petite Crau and La Grande Crau. Centuries of irrigation have created productive farmland in these arid areas – although parts of La Grande Crau revert to a stony desert in summer.

BACKGROUND

Roman Orange

Just to the west is the watery plain of the Rhône delta. By Arles the river splits into two (the Grand Rhône to the east and the Petit Rhône to the west). These two arms embrace the Camargue, with its shimmering salt marshes, lagoons and sand flats – part of which is protected as a nature reserve. This is an unspoilt land of unique character, whose spacious horizons merge with the sea along its shifting shoreline.

The Golfe de Fos, to the east of the Camargue, shows the hand of modern man at its least attractive, in the shape of oil refineries and other industrial complexes. This ugly development spreads east around the shores of the huge lake, the Etang de Berre.

East from here, the coast of Bouches-du-Rhône and Var is backed by ranges of rocky hills or mountains, with steep and thickly wooded slopes where pine and eucalyptus perfume the warm air. The highest is the Massif de la Ste-Baume, which rises east of Marseille and stretches into Var, reaching a height of 3,763 feet (1,147m). The bays along this coast are typically framed by towering hillsides or cliffs. Especially dramatic are the *calanques* found just southeast of Marseille – long, narrow inlets with sheer, rocky sides plunging into the sparkling turquoise sea.

Chains of rugged hills and mountains stretch across Provence almost to the Rhône, generally running in an east to west direction – these are part of the great folds that formed the Alps. In Bouches-du-Rhône is the evocative, rocky Chaîne des Alpilles, which juts up to 1,270 feet (387m) from the Crau plains northeast of Arles; and east of Aix, rising to 3,317 feet (1,011m) is the pale marbled ridge of Montagne Ste-Victoire, so beloved of Cézanne.

Stretching across southern Vaucluse is the long range of the Montagne du Lubéron, reaching 3,690 feet (1,125m), whose intimate, green slopes roll down to the Durance valley. In north Vaucluse looms the mighty Mont Ventoux, with dark wooded sides rising to a bare, bleak white peak at 6,263 feet (1,909m); just to its west lie the jagged, rocky crags of the Dentelles de Montmirail.

The massifs of Provence are largely composed of smoky-cream limestone. In places the high plateaux have been cut by rivers into deep and dramatic gorges, such as the Gorges de la Nesque to the north of the Plateau de Vaucluse. Even more breathtaking are the soaring cliffs of the Grand Canyon du Verdon, in the Plateau de Valensole on the border of Alpes-de-Haute-Provence and Var. The scenery becomes more spectacularly Alpine and desolate to the northeast.

Agricultural products remain close to the heart of traditional Provence, for it is France's top producer of fruit and vegetables. Vineyards, olive groves, orchards and lavender fields form a typical backdrop to the region. Even so, modern industry has gained an increasingly strong foothold, especially around the commercial hub of Marseille and the Rhône valley. Established industries such as ochre and bauxite mining have now been joined by petro-chemicals, hydroelectric and nuclear power, aeronautics and, of course, tourism.

A quiet cloister in Arles

BACKGROUND

Much of the modern development and most of the largest towns lie on or near the coast and the Rhône valley. Towards the north and east Provence becomes more sparsely inhabited. Even so, the whole of Provence abounds in lovely old villages, which seem an integral and timeless part of the landscape – some, aptly named *villages perchés,* look like a continuation of the rocky hilltops on which they are perched. Many are located in spectacular positions and enjoy superb views. Some cling to steep slopes, often in a higgledy-piggledy huddle around a castle or church, a tangled maze of tiny streets (narrow to give shade from the sun, deliberately tortuous to break the force of the wind). The mellow honey-stone buildings are topped with age-mottled terracotta pantiles and adorned with painted wooden shutters, wrought-iron lamps and a profusion of climbing plants or pots of bright flowers. All have little squares or corners with splashing fountains – and often a clock tower topped by bells within a delicate wrought-iron campanile. The old centre may well be clustered within the remains of medieval ramparts entered through old gateways; wider streets surrounding this core are typically lined

Roman theatre,
Vaison-la-Romaine

with plane trees. Some have a crumbling, traditionally rustic appeal; others have been revamped but retain their original character.

History and Culture

The history of Provence is so rich and varied that it is well worth delving more deeply into the subject than is possible in this potted version, which is intended to help put the region in perspective.

Traces of human habitation have been found here dating from the Stone Age, with more extensive evidence from the Iron and Bronze Ages when the Ligurians and Celts arrived. The Celto-Ligurians built the first stone shepherds' huts, called *bories*, and hilltop fortifications, called *oppida*. A more advanced civilisation came in 600BC when the Phocaean Greeks founded *Massalia* (Marseille). This became an influential republican city-state, due to its wealth and importance as a commercial (and intellectual) centre. The ancient Greeks introduced vines and olives, and set up other colonies along the coast. Their alliance with Rome led to a takeover by the Romans from 125BC. *Arelate* (Arles) became the main town in the area and an important commercial port. The whole of southern France, then known as *Provincia Romana*, saw great advances in agriculture, trade and culture. By the time the Roman Empire fell in AD476, it had left a profound and permanent mark on the area. Incursions by Germanic tribes followed, and the region became part of the Frankish empire – ruled for a time by Charlemagne. Bloodshed continued with raids by the Saracens (Arabs), who took control of the coast but were routed at the end of the 10th century.

The amphitheatre, Nîmes

Provence was still part of the Holy Roman Empire in the 12th century, but power over the region was delegated to feudal counts and lords, who retained a fierce grip on their fiefdoms. This was a time of conflict and instability when many villages were fortified and set on hills. It was also a period when the literary art of the troubadours flourished: they composed courtly love poems to wealthy ladies, using a language derived from the Latin spoken in Roman times – hence Provençal was

Clock tower in Aix

born. The Romans had established Christianity, and many churches and abbeys were built in this era in Romanesque style. It was also a time of renewed trade, stimulated by the Crusades. A period of stability returned in the 13th century, when the Catalan Count Raimond-Bérenger V united the region under his rule. He was succeeded by his youngest daughter, Béatrice, who married Charles of Anjou – brother of St Louis, King of France. One result was a closer link between Provence and the papacy, and in 1271 the region known as the Comtat Venaissin, in west Vaucluse, was ceded to the pope. By 1309 the feuding in Rome was such that the French Pope Clément V decided to take refuge in Avignon, where he set up the papal court. Some 40 years later, in 1348, Clément VI purchased the town of Avignon outright and founded the great Palais des Papes (Palace of the Popes). In 1377, Gregory XI was persuaded to move back to Rome, but the French cardinals elected an antipope, thus instigating the Great Schism which lasted until 1403 – although Avignon and the Comtat remained papal property until 1791.

One of the first acts of Pope Clément V was the founding of a university in Avignon and this was followed a century later, in 1409, by the establishment of the university of Aix. Not long after, in 1434, Aix was ruled by René of Anjou ('Good King René') who brought a rare period of peace during which the arts flourished and commerce was revived. In 1486, Provence then entered into a formal union with the crown of France, though retaining a degree of autonomy exercised by the Parlement de Provence, based in Aix.

The 16th century saw the birth of two notable characters who both lived in Salon: one was Nostradamus (Michel de Nostredame), a physician born in St-Rémy and renowned for his book of predictions; the other was Adam de Craponne, an engineer who built a canal to irrigate the arid Crau area. The 16th century also brought the bitter Wars of Religion, resulting in brutal conflict between the Catholic papal domains and centres of Protestantism, such as the principality of Orange (the

*Les Bories –
ancient beehive
houses near
Gordes*

property of the northern European House of
Orange-Nassau until 1713). The horrors of war
were compounded by outbreaks of plague and
political strife.

Prosperity returned in the 18th century,
stimulated by maritime commerce, and many
of the grand mansions in Marseille and Aix
date from this period.

By the end of the 18th century, however,
serious economic and social problems led to
suffering and discontent throughout Europe.
Riots erupted in Provence and the Bastille was
stormed in Paris, marking the start of the
French Revolution in 1789. The Aix parliament
had already been deprived of its powers by
the French crown. In 1790 the Assembly in
Paris divided the formerly unified Provence
into three administrative *départements*:
Bouches-du-Rhône, Var and Basses-Alpes. A
year later the papal lands were given back to
France and combined with other areas
(including Orange) to form Vaucluse. Ever
independent-minded, the people of Marseille
were staunch supporters of the Revolution, and
their battle song, *'La Marseillaise'*, came to be
adopted as the national anthem.

BACKGROUND

Fortified Trigance

Napoléon had close connections with the area (it was from Nice that he began his first military campaign) but the Napoleonic Wars eventually lost him his local support – Provence longed for its old autonomy. This desire for independence was expressed by an intellectual movement, founded in 1854 and called the Félibrige, which was dedicated to the revival of the original Provençal language; its members included the Nobel Prize-winning poet, Frédéric Mistral, who wrote romances in the language of the troubadours. The native artist Paul Cézanne and his boyhood friend, the novelist Emile Zola, returned to this area in the 1870s, and the region subsequently attracted an eminent list of painters (Renoir, Van Gogh, Gauguin and Matisse) and writers (such as Daudet). Marseille became the most important port in France, boosted by the expansion of colonial trade with Africa and the Far East. The coming of the railways soon encouraged early tourism along the Côte d'Azur, and not long afterwards travellers began discovering the delights of Provence.

Provence Today

Provence has a strong regional identity and its people are bound together by their rich local traditions and independent spirit. But within it are distinct *pays* (regions), such as the Camargue or Lubéron, which have their own individual identities. The cities also have different characters, like refined Aix and raffish Marseille, as different as chalk and cheese, though only 16 miles (25km) apart.

Noble wines

The Provençaux proudly uphold their old traditions and values, especially the older generation. Religion plays a major role here, although in many *fêtes* and local customs, pagan folklore often goes hand-in-hand with Christian beliefs. The Provençal language is rarely spoken – but it is used, for example, on signs to indicate the alternative name for towns and villages. Locals may seem wary of visitors at first, but once the ice is broken they are very friendly and hospitable.

Much of Provence still has a rural atmosphere, but now only a small proportion of people work on the land (10 per cent in 1982). Farms tend to be small, family-run concerns – as they were centuries ago – and communities often have agricultural co-operatives, especially for the production and marketing of the local wine.

At the same time, Provence is far from insular. This century has seen the arrival of a new wave of luminaries: artists such as Picasso and Cocteau and writers such as Colette, Scott Fitzgerald and Somerset Maugham. On a local level today, this 'arty' ambience has generated a plethora of little shops selling paintings, pottery and sculpture.

The appeal of the area has brought other kinds of settlers – bohemians seeking the simple life,

A shady square

glitterati (from rock stars to royalty) indulging their jet-set tastes, students from many countries, northerners seeking a holiday home in the sun and, sadly, gangsters involved in organised crime.

The coast has always attracted a cosmopolitan mix of people, most notably Marseille which now has a large North African population. The region has deep political divisions, and racism has fuelled recent support for the far right, despite years of staunch socialism. North Africans are not the first to suffer hatred: in the past this was directed at Jewish inhabitants (who enjoyed papal protection in the Comtat until the 16th century), at Protestants and at immigrants from Spain and Italy.

The Rhône valley and the coast, with their busy towns and resorts, presents a sharp contrast to the more sparsely populated inland areas. Here you will find timeless, traditional rural villages and plenty of quiet, unspoilt spots well off the beaten track. Even so, tourism has moved in during recent years, and many old buildings have been revamped to make bijou second homes (probably saving some villages from extinction). The results of tourism are not always so benign. Well-known historic towns and villages are often wall-to-wall with visitors in summer, detracting from their evocative atmosphere, and truly rustic Provence is very hard to find in August. To discover the real spirit of Provence it is best to visit in spring, early summer or autumn.

Provence caters for affluent visitors, so overall it tends to be expensive – do not expect many bargains. The Mediterranean lifestyle does mean, however, that there are lots of lively pavement cafés, and everyone stops for a long lunch-break and siesta. You will not find much nightlife away from the coast, but you certainly will find a wide choice of restaurants serving wonderful Provençal fare – so you can eat, drink and be merry, and even join in a traditional game of *boules*.

In summary, Provence boasts the best of all that the French hold most dear to their spiritual hearts – art and culture, food and wine, sunshine and style – in a setting that is both beautiful and historic.

What to See

The Essential rating system:

✓	'top ten'

♦♦♦ do not miss
♦♦   see if you can
♦   worth seeing if
        you have time

There is an enormous amount to see and do in Provence, and you will have a more rewarding holiday if you select one area and get to know it well rather than dashing from point to point. Consequently this section of the guide has been divided into eight main regions, each of which can be explored, at a leisurely pace, over a period of two to three days. These regions are described in an anti-clockwise direction, starting with Vaucluse. This *département* has been divided into four main areas – west Vaucluse, the southern mountains of the Lubéron, the central Plateau de Vaucluse and north Vaucluse, dominated by Mont Ventoux. All four areas are rich in historic and cultural highlights.

Next we move southwards to look at west Bouches-du-Rhône, centred around Arles, the Camargue, and east Bouches-du-Rhône with its two major cities of Aix and Marseille. Finally we move east for a brief look at the mountainous expanse of Var and Alpes-de-Haut-Provence, a region of majestic landscapes and timeless old villages.

Châteauneuf-du-Pape

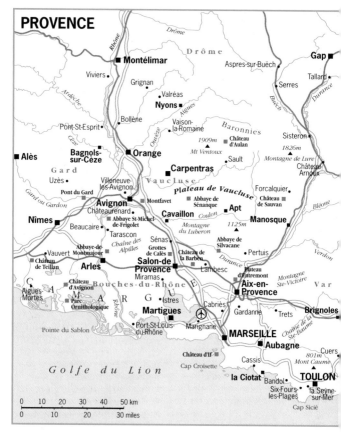

PROVENCE

Drôme

Drôme

Gap ■

■ Montélimar

Aspres-sur-Buëch •

Tallard •

Viviers •

Grignan •

Serres •

Valréas •

Nyons ■

Aigues

Bollène •

Vaison-la-Romaine •

Baronnies

Sisteron ■

Pont-St-Esprit •

1909▲
Mt Ventoux

Château
d'Aulan ■

1826▲
Montagne de Lure

Château
d'Arnoux ■

Alès ■

Bagnols-
sur-Cèze

■ Orange

Carpentras

• Sault

Gard

Vaucluse

Uzès •

Villeneuve-
les-Avignon

plateau de Vaucluse

Forcalquier •

Château
de Sauvan ■

Bléone

Pont du Gard

Avignon ■

Montfavet •

Abbaye de
Sénanque ■

Apt ■

Manosque ■

Châteaurenard •

Cavaillon ■

Coulon

1125▲

Gard ou Gardon

Nîmes ■

Abbaye St-Michel-
de-Frigolet ■

Montagne
du Luberon

Beaucaire •

Tarascon •

Sénas •

Abbaye de
Silvacane ■

Verdon

Chaîne des
Alpilles

Grottes
de Calès

Château de
la Barben ■

• Pertuis

Abbaye de
Montmajour ■

Vauvert •

Salon-de-
Provence

Durance

Château
de Teillan ■

Arles ■

Miramas •

Lambesc •

Plateau
d'Entremont ■

Montagne
Ste-Victoire

Aix-en-
Provence ■

Var

C

Château
d'Avignon ■

Bouches-du-Rhône

Cabriès •

Gardanne •

• Trets

Brignoles ■

Aigues-
Mortes

A

M

A

R

G

U

E

Istres •

Parc
Ornithologique

Martigues ■

Marignane •

Montagne de la
Ste-Baume

Rhône

Pointe du Sablon

Port-St-Louis-
du-Rhône

MARSEILLE ■

Aubagne ■

Cuers •

801▲
Mont Caume

Château d'If ■

Cassis •

Golfe   du   Lion

Cap Croisette

la Ciotat ■

Bandol •

TOULON ■

Six-Fours-
les-Plages

la Seyne-
sur-Mer

Cap Sicié

| 0 | 10 | 20 | 30 | 40 | 50 km |

| 0 | 10 | 20 | 30 miles |

WEST VAUCLUSE

The *département* of Vaucluse is bordered to the west by the wide, stately Rhône, which has always been a major communication route. Today one of France's busiest highways, the Autoroute du Soleil, leads south into Provence along the river valley. For a long time the Rhône formed a frontier between independent Provence and the Kingdom of France, and medieval border fortifications still stand defiantly on both sides of the river – most notably at Avignon. The valley is also the setting for the historic town of Orange, with its well-preserved Roman monuments. More recently, modern industry has developed along the Rhône. Stretching eastwards from the river is the Comtat Venaissin, a fertile and intensively cultivated plain known as the Garden of France.

This is also an important wine-making region, most famous for the deep red vintages of Châteauneuf-du-Pape.

AVIGNON ✓

After the papal court was set up in Avignon in the 14th century, the clergy lived in luxury, ostentatiously displaying their wealth and power. This glittering city hummed with highlife and low – the Italian poet Petrarch described it as: 'Unholy Babylon... sink of iniquity'.

Today Avignon is big and busy – certainly not a restful place to stay, but the sights make it a must on any tourist itinerary. It also has numerous stylish shops. Devotion to art and culture burns as brightly today as in the past and Avignon explodes with life and colour during the summer festival, when it overflows with visitors. The core of Avignon, known as the Vieille Ville (Old Town) is enclosed by fortified walls, built by the papacy, and dominated by the towers of the cathedral and of the majestic Palais des Papes. The Rhône skirts the north and west walls of the old town and the views from this side are splendid – as they must have been centuries ago. Jutting into the river here are the remains of Pont St-Bénézet, the medieval bridge made famous by the song ('*Sur le pont d'Avignon...*'). On the opposite bank stands the mighty fortress of Villeneuve-lès-Avignon (see page 35). Avignon's medieval ramparts stretch for a total of 3 miles (4.8km) and surround a maze of narrow streets, lined with grand palaces and noble mansions dating from the 14th to the 18th centuries. Even so, none of these buildings can compare for sheer splendour with the **Palais des Papes**, set in a spacious cobbled square to the north of the old town. Lying behind it is the 12th-century cathedral of **Notre-Dame-des-Doms** and the lovely **Rocher des Doms** gardens clinging to a

The Old Town, Avignon

rocky bluff offering fine views. Just south of the Place du Palais is the large **Place de l'Horloge**, lined with plane trees and pavement cafés – a lively spot, especially in the early evening when buskers and artists ply their trade. Leading south from this square is the main shopping street, the busy **Rue de la République**. This runs into **Cours Jean-Jaurès**, where the tourist office is located in a mansion (No 41) beside the old church and ruined cloister of St-Martial, with its restful public garden.

Some of the finest mansions (*hôtels*) lie in the area around the Palais des Papes, including the 17th-century **Hôtel des Monnaies** (the old mint, now the Music Conservatory) with its baroque façade. Another, close to the Rue de la République, is the 15th-century **Palais du Roure** (a centre for Provençal studies), which has carved wooden doors opening on to a pretty cobbled courtyard. Nearby is one of

Avignon's oldest churches, the 14th-century Gothic **St-Agricol**. There are more handsome 17th and 18th-century *hôtels* along the chic **Rue Joseph-Vernet**, along **Rue Banasterie**, near the Palais, and along **Rue du Roi René**. Also in the Rue du Roi René is the 14th-century church of **St-Didier**, in true Provençal Gothic style with original frescos. Close by is the **Médiathèque Ceccano**, the city library, housed in a 14th-century palace. Further north, on Place Carnot, is the 14th-century church of **St-Pierre**, with its remarkable Renaissance doorway. Avignon has numerous attractive squares whose open-air cafés and restaurants are often shaded by trees. Wandering around, you will also come across peaceful corners away from the main streets, especially to the east. One such spot is **Rue des Teinturiers**, a picturesque cobbled street with the Sorgue river flowing along one side. Here you will see old mill wheels, a reminder of the city's once-important cloth industry. The fine 16th-century **Chapelle des Pénitents-Gris** can be reached over one of the wrought-iron footbridges that cross the Sorgue.

◆ CATHEDRALE NOTRE-DAME-DES-DOMS

Place du Palais
Avignon's cathedral dates from the 12th century, with later alterations, and Romanesque gives way to baroque in the cavernous interior. The belfry was adorned with its tasteless gilded Virgin in the 19th century. The impressive Gothic style tomb of Pope Jean XXII lies inside.

◆◆ MUSEE CALVET

65 Rue J-Vernet
This splendid 18th-century palace contains a fascinating collection of art, antiquities and artefacts.

◆ MUSEE LOUIS VOULAND

17 Rue Victor-Hugo
This museum houses a fine display of 17th and 18th-century French decorative art which includes marquetry furniture, porcelain, silver, Provençal pottery and oriental *objets*.
Open: June to September, Tuesday to Saturday 10.00–12.00 and 14.00–18.00hrs; October to May, Tuesday to Saturday 14.00–18.00hrs. *Closed:* Sunday and Monday.

◆◆ MUSEE DU PETIT PALAIS

Place du Palais
This suitably grand 14th-century archbishop's palace houses a rich collection of medieval and Renaissance works of art (mostly Italian and Avignon schools).
Open: Wednesday to Monday 09.30–11.50 and 14.00–18.00hrs. *Closed:* Tuesday.

◆ MUSEE THEODORE AUBANEL

Place St-Pierre
The author Théodore Aubanel did much to preserve the Provençal language. His family home displays manuscripts, drawings and letters and a small museum of printing.
Open: Monday to Friday 09.00–12.00hrs. *Closed:* Saturday, Sunday and August.

◆◆◆ PALAIS DES PAPES

Place du Palais
The grandiose 14th-century papal palace was built like a feudal fortress with massive stone walls and awe-inspiring towers. Through the grand Porte des Champeaux is the great inner courtyard (used as a setting for festival events), dividing the two parts of the huge palace; the simple Romanesque Palais Vieux (Old Palace) was built by Pope Benoit XII from 1334, and the Gothic Palais Nouveau (New Palace) by his successor Clément VI from 1342.
The magnificent halls and chambers are now empty of the sumptuous furnishings of papal times, giving a false impression

of austerity – though there are some fine frescos in the Chapelles St-Jean and St-Martial, and in Clément VI's bedroom and study.

Open: daily; guided tours (lasting 1 hour), April to June and October, 09.00–12.15 and 14.00–18.00hrs; July to September, 09.00–19.00hrs; November to March, 09.00–12.15 and 14.00–17.15hrs.

PONT ST-BENEZET

From the medieval Châtelet tower on the ramparts you can walk (or dance) on the remains of the famous 12th-century bridge, with its little chapel. Legend has it that the song about the bridge goes back to the time when thieves danced on the island beneath (*sous* rather than *sur* le pont) as potential victims walked above. *Open:* April to September, daily 09.00 –18.30hrs; October to March, daily 09.00– 17.00hrs except Monday.

Two other museums are the **Musée Lapidaire** (27 Rue de la République), with archaeological exhibits (closed Tuesday), and the **Musée Requien** (67 Rue J-Vernet) of natural history (closed Sunday and Monday).

Accommodation

Apart from a good choice of hotels in the centre, the suburbs offer quieter alternatives – as does Villeneuve-lès-Avignon (see page 35) and the Ile de la Barthelasse, a large flat rural island in the Rhône, near the city centre, which also has campsites.

In the Old Town

Very beautiful and ultra-expensive, **La Mirande**, 4 Place de l'Amirande (tel: 90 85 93 93), is set in a medieval cardinal's palace by the Palais. The expensive **Europe**, 12 Place Crillon (tel: 90 82 66 92), is elegant and full of antiques. Among more moderately-priced hotels is the **Danieli**, 17 Rue de la République (tel: 90 86 46 82), in a fine old building with airy modern decor. The following hotels all have rooms at reasonable or low rates. **Palais des Papes**, 1 Rue Gérard-Philipe (tel: 90 86 04 13), just off the Place du Palais; wooden beams, traditional furnishings and a popular restaurant. **De Mons**, 5 Rue de Mons (tel: 90 82 57 16); in a little 13th-century chapel with vaulted stone walls just off the Place de l'Horloge. **Le Mediéval**, 15 Rue Petite Saunerie (tel: 90 86 11 06); an old building with a pretty plant-filled patio (self-catering studios available for stays of a week or more). **Mignon**, 12 Rue J-Vernet (tel: 90 82 17 30); basic with chintzy touches.

In the Surroundings

Very expensive, calm and comfortable, **Les Frênes**, 645 Ave les Vertes-Rives, Montfavet (tel: 90 31 17 93), is a classic large French house, tastefully furnished and set in a tree-lined garden with a pool. The expensive **Auberge de Cassagne**, 450 Allée de Cassagne, Le Pontet (tel: 90 31 04 18), is a traditional Provençal house, full of appeal and character, set in beautiful

The Palais des Papes

gardens with a pool. A *Logis* at very reasonable rates is **Auberge de Bonpas**, Route de Cavaillon, Montfavet (tel: 90 23 07 64), an old-fashioned stone house set in a shady garden.

Eating Out

The old town is full of restaurants to suit all pockets and tastes – from grand gourmet establishments to burger bars. There is a good choice of pavement café/brasseries serving simple meals on Rue de la République, Place de l'Horloge and other squares in the central pedestrian zone, such as Place du Change. The northwest quarter has many of the more upmarket restaurants, including the hotels **La Mirande** and **Europe** (see above), which are highly recommended.

In the old town, higher-priced restaurants include **Christian Etienne**, 10 Rue de Mons, which has a terrace overlooking the Palais; it is sophisticated but relaxed, with stylish modern decor and imaginative cuisine to match (vegetarian menu available). **Brunel**, 46 Rue de la Balance, is one of Avignon's best, thanks to the delicious choice of creative dishes; it has a glass-covered terrace (vegetarian menu available; closed Sunday). The venerable **Hiély-Lucullus**, 5 Rue de la République, is a very traditional restaurant, where devotion to the wonderful Provençal cuisine is all (closed Monday).

A moderately-priced set menu can be found at **Le Vernet**, 58

Rue J-Vernet, a handsome townhouse with a walled garden and tables under the trees, where the fish is very good (special dishes for children). Lower-priced menus can also be found at the following restaurants. **Café des Artistes**, Place Crillon, has chic 1930s-style decor and a lively cuisine (closed Sunday and Monday). **Le Jardin de la Tour**, 9 Rue de la Tour, is an old factory with original machinery and awnings over the courtyard dining area, offering simple fare

(closed Sunday). **Le Bain Marie**, 5 Rue Pétramale, set in a delightful, cool, plant-filled patio, serves light and tasty dishes (closed Saturday lunch and Sunday). **Le Saint-Pierre**, 10 Pl St-Pierre, has tables on the cobbled square facing the church and typical French cuisine (very good value lunch menu; closed Saturday lunch and Monday). **Les Trois Clefs**, 26 Rue des Trois-Faucons, is a relaxed bistro decorated with murals, where inventive local dishes include fish (children's

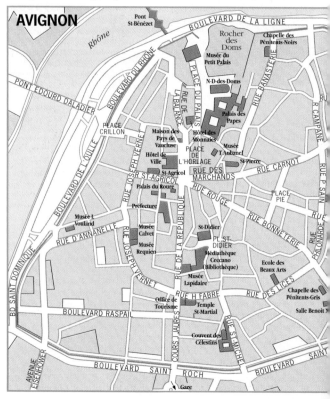

A typically relaxed pavement café in the Place de l'Horloge, Avignon's main square

menu; closed Sunday). **Notre Dame**, 34 Rue Four-de-la-Terre, is a charming rustic inn in traditional Languedoc style, just like the delicious and filling food (closed Sunday).

For daytime snacks and delicious teas try **Les Félibres**, 14–16 Rue du Limas, a refined and pretty *salon de thé* with wood panelling and bookshelves; it also sells books on Provence, cookery, homes and gardens (closed Monday in July to September).

Nightlife

Galaxy, 23 Route de Montfavet, is a popular disco. **Club 5.5**, Porte St-Roch, is a cabaret-dance venue for the more mature crowd. **AJMI Jazz Club**, Théâtre du Chêne Noir, 8 Bis Rue Ste-Catherine, has live music – as do cafés like **La Jamaique**, 24 Bis Rue St-Etienne, and **La Tâche d'Encre**, 22 Rue des Teinturiers.

WEST VAUCLUSE

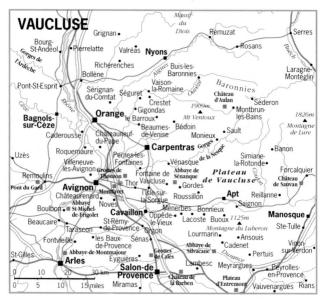

VAUCLUSE

Massif du Diois · Rémuzat · Serres
Grignan · Rosans
Bourg-St-Andéol · Pierrelatte · Valréas · **Nyons**
Richerenches · Buis-les-Baronnies · Laragne-Montéglin
Bollène · Vaison-la-Romaine · *Baronnies*
Pont-St-Esprit · Sérignan-du-Comtat · Séguret · Crestet · Château d'Aulan · Séderon
Cèze · Gigondas · *1909m* Mt Ventoux · Montbrun-les-Bains · *1826m*
Orange · le Barroux · Beaumes-de-Venise · Bédoin · Monieux · Sault · *Montagne de Lure*
Bagnols-sur-Cèze · Châteauneuf-du-Pape · *Gorges* · Banon
Caderousse · **CARPENTRAS** · *de la Nesque* · Simiane-la-Rotonde · Forcalquier
Uzès · Roquemaure · Pernes-les-Fontaines · Vénasque · Abbaye de Sénanque · *Plateau de Vaucluse* · Château de Sauvan
Remoulins · Villeneuve-les-Avignon · Grottes de Thouzon · Fontaine de Vaucluse · Gordes
Pont du Gard · **Avignon** · le Thor · L'Isle-sur-la-Sorgue · Roussillon · **Apt** · Reillanne
Châteaurenard · Montfavet · Saignon
Abbaye St-Michel-de-Frigolet · Noves · Ménerbes · Bonnieux · *1125m* · **Manosque**
Boulbon · Cavaillon · St-Rémy-de-Provence · Oppède-le-Vieux · Lacoste Buoux · *Montagne du Luberon* · Ste-Tulle
Beaucaire · Tarascon · Orgon · Lourmarin · Ansouis · Vinon-sur-Verdon
Fontvieille · les Baux-de-Provence · Sénas · Abbaye de Silvacane · Cadenet · Pertuis · Peyrolles-en-Provence
St-Gilles · Abbaye-de-Montmajour · Eyguières · Grottes de Calès · Lambesc · Meyrargues · Vauvenargues · Rians
Arles · **Salon-de-Provence** · *Durance* · Plateau d'Entremont
Miramas · Château de la Barben

0 10 20 30 km
0 5 10 15 miles

Shopping

Avignon is a very popular shopping centre, with lots of lovely shops in the old town – but prices tend to be high. **Rue de la République** is the main shopping street, with some of the more moderately-priced larger stores; well-known names include Monoprix, Galeries Lafayette and Habitat.

Just to the west is **Rue Joseph-Vernet**, with the smartest shops in town – it has many fashion boutiques where designer labels abound (even in children's shops) at sky-high prices. One shop to look out for here is **Souleiado**, famous for its traditional Provençal fabrics which are used to make anything from clothes to furnishings; their colourful prints also decorate a wide range of goods (such as towels, crockery and washbags). **Puyricard** has a too-tempting array of luxurious chocolates (made in Aix), reputed to be among the best in France. Rue Joseph-Vernet and others in the upmarket northwest quarter also offer a good choice of antique shops.

In Rue St-Agricol, a little street between Rue J-Vernet and Place de l'Horloge, you will find **Ducs de Gascogne** selling traditional food and drink specialities in tasteful packaging. There are also two mouth-watering sweet shops and even the two fruit and vegetable shops here are stylish, with colourful displays of unusual produce.

In Rue Petite Fusterie, a street running north, is **Hervé Baume**, a treasure trove of *objets* for the house and garden, modern and antique, chic and rustic, practical and pretty, including pottery, glassware, baskets and furniture.

In Rue de la Balance, nearer the Palais, **La Taste** sells Provençal crafts and souvenirs, such as pottery, printed skirts and shirts, wines, herbs, toilet water and dried flowers.

The busy, narrow streets in the central pedestrian zone are lined with a wide variety of shops, including branches of Benetton and Stefanel and other clothes boutiques that are less pricey than those in Rue J-Vernet. Along the north side, in Rue des Marchands, **Les Olivades** is another shop famous for its Provençal fabrics and a range of other items made to traditional designs.

Avignon has several lively **markets**: bric-a-brac in Place Crillon (Saturday); a flea market in Place des Carmes (Sunday morning); a flower market in Place des Carmes (Saturday morning); general stalls along Rempart St-Michel (Saturday and Sunday morning); and Les Halles, a covered market with a huge array of food, in Place Pie (Tuesday to Sunday mornings).

Special Events
The **Festival of Dramatic Art** (July and August) includes theatre, film, dance, music and fringe events – for information contact Maison Jean Vilar, 8 Rue de Mons (tel: 90 82 67 08).

The chapel on the 12th-century Pont St-Bénézet

◆◆

CARPENTRAS

This busy market town is set on the shady banks of the river Auzon, in the midst of rich farmland, with the bold silhouette of Mont Ventoux to the northeast. It became the capital of the Comtat Venaissin in 1320 and, under the protection of the popes, had a sizeable Jewish ghetto.

Today it has a lively, attractive old centre, surrounded by plane-lined avenues. On the north side is a vestige of the medieval ramparts, the hefty, crenellated **Porte d'Orange**. By a restful square at the heart of the old town is the 17th-century **Palais de Justice**, an Italianate episcopal palace with original friezes inside. A Roman **Arc de Triomphe** is tucked in the courtyard behind. Next to it is the large, mainly Gothic **Cathédrale St-Siffrein**, dating from the 15th century, with its striking doorway, Porte Juive, through which converted Jews entered the church.

France's oldest synagogue, the **Maison de Prières**, lies nearby in Place Maurice Charretier; it has an elegant interior where you can see the purification baths and bread ovens (*open:* Monday to Friday 10.00–12.00hrs and 15.00–17.00hrs). On Boulevard Albin-Durand is a mansion with two museums: the **Comtadin** displays artefacts to do with local history, such as bells used on sheep drives, and the **Duplessis** houses art, including Renaissance

Orange, the best-preserved Roman theatre in France

miniatures, plus a library with an important collection of Provençal books. It is also worth visiting the opulent old pharmacy in the 18th-century hospital, **Hôtel-Dieu**, in Place Aristide-Briand (*open:* Monday, Wednesday and Thursday mornings).

Accommodation

The **Hôtel du Fiacre**, 153 Rue Vigne (tel: 90 63 03 15), is an 18th-century mansion in a quiet street, with period decor, a pretty courtyard and rooms at very reasonable rates.

Eating Out

Two simple, intimate little restaurants offering moderately priced *nouvelle cuisine* are **Le Vert Galant**, 12 Rue de Clapies (closed Saturday lunch and Sunday) and **L'Orangerie**, 26 Rue Duplessis (closed Saturday lunch). **La Saule Pleureur**, 145 Chemin de Beauregard, Monteux, southwest of Carpentras, has a garden terrace and a restaurant with an excellent reputation, serving delicious dishes with a local flavour, at rather higher prices (closed Tuesday evening and Wednesday).

Shopping

The arcaded **Rue des Halles** and other streets are full of colour on Friday, when the market takes over the old town – in winter there is also a famous truffle market. Local crafts and food are sold at **La Tonnelle** in Passage Boyer, a 19th-century glass-covered arcade. Look out for the local caramel sweets called *berlingots*.

WEST VAUCLUSE

◆
CAVAILLON
The name of this major market town is synonymous with a variety of small sweet melon which is grown in the surrounding fields. In the old centre, the Romanesque **Cathédrale Notre-Dame-et-St-Véran** has a charming, weathered 13th-century cloister; one chapel has a painting of St-Véran chasing off a legendary local monster. The **Musée Judeo-Comtadin**, in an old bakery on Rue Hébraique, tells the story of the town's Jewish community. The **Musée Archéologique**, in the old Hôtel-Dieu, includes Iron-Age finds from the rocky hill St-Jacques, just west of the old town, worth climbing for its old chapel and lovely views.

Accommodation
Hôtel du Parc, Place du Clos (tel: 90 71 57 78) is agreeably old-fashioned and very reasonably priced.

Eating Out
Fin de Siècle, Place du Clos, is a period-style restaurant, popular for crayfish and its low-priced menus (children's menu; closed Wednesday). **Prévot**, 353 Avenue de Verdun, towards the outskirts, serves creative dishes using local products, with moderate to expensive menus (closed Sunday evening and Monday). **Nicolet**, Route de Pertuis, Cheval-Blanc, southeast of Cavaillon, is modern and airy with a terrace looking over the Lubéron, offering moderate to expensive Provençal cuisine (closed Sunday evening and Monday).

Shopping
There is a lively market on Monday in **Place du Clos** (the town also boasts the second-largest wholesale fruit and vegetable market in France, Monday to Saturday). For stylish crafts and antiques, try **Victoria en Provence**, 139 Cours Gambetta.

◆
CHATEAUNEUF-DU-PAPE
A green sea of vines rolls across the undulating countryside around this large village which produces the Rhône valley's most prestigious wine. It was first made famous by Pope Jean XXII, who built his summer residence here and planted the vineyards. The village itself consists of mellow sandstone buildings climbing the slopes of a hill, crowned by the ruins of the 14th-century papal château.
There is no mistaking that wine is the main business here. Free tasting is offered by numerous *domaines* and *caveaux*, including some grand old places (the tourist office has lists). Various Rhône wines can be tasted at Père Anselme's **Musée des Outils de Vignerons**, where historic wine-making equipment is displayed (open daily 09.00–12.00 and 14.00–18.00hrs, closed January and February). You can also visit *caves* along the pretty Route des Vins (which follows the D92 road).

◆
L'ISLE-SUR-LA-SORGUE
The old centre of this green and pleasant town is almost an island, embraced by the arms

of the river Sorgue, which flows around and through it. The river once turned the wheels of the cloth and silk mills which brought prosperity to the town. The mills closed long ago, but the weed-filled streams still have several mossy waterwheels as a reminder. At the heart of the old quarter is a 17th-century **church** with a rich baroque interior. Next door is a fine 18th-century granary that now houses the tourist office, and nearby is the **Hôtel Donadei de Campredon**, which is an art gallery. The **Hôtel-Dieu**, an 18th-century hospital, has a pharmacy with porcelain pots and curious potions.

Nearby
Le Thor, a small town to the west, has a fine Romanesque church and medieval belfry. Also nearby are the caves of the **Grottes de Thouzon** (*open*: daily April to September, Sunday only March and November; *closed*: December to February).

Fine regional wines with a papal pedigree

Accommodation and Eating Out
La Gueulardière, 1 Avenue Jean-Charmasson (tel: 90 38 10 52), is a *Logis* in a traditional creeper-clad building, with dining tables set round a fountain outside, and very reasonable room rates. **Mas de Cure Bourse**, Route de Caumon (tel: 90 38 16 58), just southwest of L'Isle, is a simple farmhouse with many pretty touches and a terrace overlooking the garden and pool; prices are moderate to expensive but the restaurant has a good-value menu.

Shopping
L'Isle is a hive of activity on Saturday and Sunday, when there is a great antique and flea market. There is also a general market on Sunday morning with all sorts of diverting stalls. **Sous L'Olivier**, Rue de la République, has a selection of traditional food and wine.

◆◆◆ ORANGE ✓

This large market town, by the river Meyne, was a major city in Roman times. In the Middle Ages the town and surrounding area formed an independent principality, held, until 1713, by the House of Orange-Nassau, whose princes played a major role in northern European affairs.

Today Orange is known as the gateway to Provence, so it seems appropriate that the main road from the north passes the massive, three-arched Roman **Arc de Triomphe**, decorated with sculpted friezes. Heavy traffic lumbers along this main road but the old town offers serene tree-lined squares, animated pavement cafés and lovely old buildings. Rising above the town, to the south, is the **Parc de la Colline St-Eutrope** – a large terraced park set on a hill from which there are bird's eye views of the town and beyond. The park contains the ruins of a château built by the Princes of Orange, as well as a campsite and swimming pool. At its foot lies the magnificent **Théâtre Antique**, the best-preserved Roman theatre in France. The auditorium once held 10,000 spectators, and it is still used to stage many events (*open:* April to September, daily 09.00–18.00hrs, October to March, daily 09.00–12.30 and 13.30–17.00hrs). Alongside the Théâtre are the excavated remains of Roman temples and villas. The old building opposite, the **Musée d'Orange**, shows local history, archaeological artefacts and paintings (open same hours as the Théâtre). On the spacious Place Clemenceau, near the centre, is the Romanesque **Cathédrale Notre-Dame**, and the Hôtel de Ville, with a 17th-century belfry.

Shops in the old town sell stylish crafts and household items and there is a general market on Thursday.

Nearby

Some 5 miles (8km) northeast of Orange, in **Sérignan**, is **L'Harmas**, the home of the 19th-century natural historian, J H Fabre; this charming museum, with its wild garden, displays his bright watercolour paintings of local fungi and his insect specimens (*closed:* Tuesday and October).

Accommodation

Le Mas des Aigras, Chemin des Aigras (tel: 90 34 81 01), north of Orange, is a simple and quiet farmhouse, with a flowery garden and pool, offering rooms at moderate prices.

◆ VENASQUE

Venasque is a picturesque village perched on a sheer, rocky spur on the northwest slopes of the Plateau de Vaucluse, with views of Mont Ventoux. Surrounded by green wooded hills, vineyards and cherry orchards (there is a daily **cherry market** in May and June), Venasque stands above the plains of the Comtat Venaissin – to which it gave its name, being the episcopal seat before Carpentras. The old stone village has a quiet, unspoilt air. At the back of the 13th-century **Eglise de Notre-Dame** is a 6th-century baptistry, one of France's oldest religious buildings (*closed:* Sunday morning, Wednesday and February).

Accommodation

Uphill from the church is the **Auberge La Fontaine** (tel: 90 66 02 96), a charming hotel in an old building full of simple style and unpretentious character. Prices are high, but the menu is good value.

◆◆
VILLENEUVE-LES-AVIGNON
This quiet town, built up a wooded, rocky hill on the west bank of the Rhône (in the *département* of Gard), is connected by bridge to Avignon. It is very peaceful compared with its neighbour, which it serves as a residential district – as it did in the Middle Ages, when cardinals built luxury villas here.

A pretty street leads uphill from the town square to the mighty **Fort St-André**, built by the French king to defy the papal stronghold across the river, of which there are wonderful views (*open:* July and August, daily 10.00–19.30 hrs). Here too is the great **Chartreuse du Val de Bénédiction**, a huge Carthusian monastery full of atmosphere, and unadorned apart from some 14th-century frescos in one of the chapels. Other sights include the medieval **Eglise Collegiale**

Roman theatre, Orange

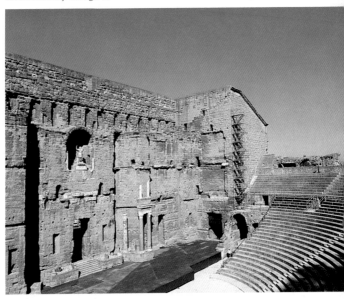

The magnificent Pont du Gard, which once brought water to Nîmes

Notre-Dame (and cloister), the **Musée Municipal** in a grand cardinal's mansion (with paintings from the Chartreuse and a rare ivory Virgin), and the **Tour Philippe-le-Bel**, built to guard the French end of Pont St-Bénézet, with fine views.

Nearby

About 14 miles (22km) west of Villeneuve (in the Languedoc region) is one of the most impressive feats of Roman engineering, the majestic **Pont du Gard**, an aqueduct carried by three tiers of arches straddling a gorge. It once carried water to Nîmes, but you can now walk across, a dizzying 150 feet (46m) above the waters of the River Gard, (or Gardon). The water came from near **Uzès**, 10 miles (16km) northwest, a sleepy, mellow medieval hill town with some interesting buildings; just outside is **Musée 1900**, a jolly exhibition of vintage cars, traction engines and toys.

The busy town of Nîmes, southwest of the Pont du Gard, has two outstanding Roman monuments: the Arènes (amphitheatre) and the temple known as the Maison Carrée.

Accommodation

Two expensive hotels with beautiful gardens, dining terraces and pools, are the **Hostellerie du Prieuré**, 7 Place du Châpitre (tel: 90 25 18 20), a tranquil priory with antique furnishings, and **La Magnaneraie**, 37 Rue Camp de Bataille (tel: 90 25 11 11), a 15th-century stone building on the outskirts. Less expensive hotels include **L'Atelier**, 5 Rue de la Foire (tel: 90 25 01 84), and **Les Cèdres**, 39 Boulevard Pasteur (tel: 90 25 43 92) with a pool; on the Ile de la Barthelasse, **La Ferme Jamet** (tel: 90 86 16 74) is a 16th-century farmhouse with a pool.

LUBERON

The *département* of Vaucluse is
bordered to the south by the
long, hump-backed ridge of the
Montagne du Lubéron. This
ridge is broken at one point by
the deep, rocky Combe de
Lourmarin, which divides the
Petit Lubéron in the west from
the Grand Lubéron in the east.
The highest peaks are in the
east where the folded crest
reaches its summit at Mourre
Nègre (3,690 feet/1,125m).
From here the panoramas are
spectacular, but from every one
of the hillsides in the area you
can enjoy a kaleidoscope of
splendid views.
The verdant, vineyard-
chequered lower slopes and
valleys of the region have a
mellow, intimate appeal. Wine-
tasting is advertised along
many winding lanes, especially
in the south – where the hills
roll gently down to the wide
Durance valley. Towards the
upper slopes the scenery
becomes much more rugged
and dramatic, with bare
limestone crags or cliffs rising
among the forests.
Altogether, Lubéron has some
of the most delightful scenery
and enchanting medieval hill
villages of all Provence – no
wonder well-heeled
northerners have chosen to
settle or buy second homes
here. Following their facelifts,
these gentrified villages can
look almost too perfectly pretty,
but they still have much original
character.
A large part of this region has
been designated as the Parc
Naturel Régional du Lubéron,
where the unspoilt beauty and
wildlife benefit from protection.
This is a marvellous area for
hiking and horse-riding. Its
pastoral peace also appeals to
artists, and there are many little
art galleries and craft shops.
For a taste of authentic
Provence, do not miss the
villages' colourful weekly
markets, or the local *fêtes*.

◆◆
ANSOUIS
This is a charming, sleepy
village of mellow stone houses
and steep, cobbled streets. The
impressive and richly furnished
château, with its terraced
gardens, dates back to the 10th
century, and is still lived in by
the Duc de Sabran. (*open:*
afternoons; *closed:* Tuesday in
winter). Nearby (Rue du Vieux
Moulin), in an old house
decorated with whimsical
sculptures, is the **Musée
Extraordinaire**; here the deep-
sea diver Georges Mazoyer
has his eclectic collection.
(*open:* afternoons). Just
northeast, amid woods and
vineyards, lies the **Etang de
Bonde**, a peaceful little lake
which is a pleasant place to
enjoy a cooling swim.

Industrial relic

LUBERON

Accommodation

By the ancient ramparts is **Le Jardin d'Ansouis** (tel: 90 09 89 27), an old stone house with a civilised ambience and lovely garden; it has two rooms at low prices, and is a pretty place for lunch or tea.

APT

This busy town, famous for crystallised fruits (*fruits confits*) and jam, has a traditional old quarter lying beside the Coulon river, with newer parts climbing the foothills either side. In Place Jean-Jaurès is the **Maison du Parc**, where you can find out all about the beautiful Parc Naturel Régional du Lubéron, including its flora and fauna, historic sights, footpaths and sports. The same building houses the **Musée de Paléontologie** with fossils and prehistoric creatures displayed in ways to make it fun for children (*open:* 08.30–12.00hrs and 14.00–18.00hrs (19.00hrs in summer); *closed:* Sunday and Tuesday). At the heart of the old town is the 12th-century **Ancienne Cathédrale Ste-Anne**, with a Romanesque crypt and valuable relics. It sits on the site of a much older church, which itself sits on the foundations of a Roman temple; local finds show this was one of the first organised Christian communities in Roman Gaul. In an 18th-century mansion nearby is the **Musée Archéologie**, which includes Roman artefacts and traditional pottery (*closed:* Sunday morning and Tuesday). West of Apt lies a fine Roman bridge, the **Pont Julien**.

Accommodation

Mas de la Tour, Gargas (tel: 90 74 12 10) is a peaceful, 12th-century farmhouse *Logis* with a pool, lying just northwest of Apt and looking over the Lubéron, offering simple rooms at reasonable rates.

Eating Out

Bernard Mathys Restaurant, Le Chêne, Gargas, in an old house with a shady garden, offers moderate and expensive menus of *nouvelle cuisine* (closed Tuesday and Wednesday).

Shopping

Apt has a good choice of shops selling local specialities, such as sweets and lavender water. The streets buzz with life, music and colourful local characters during the Saturday **market**, where you will find an extravagant array of Provençal foods and crafts. There is also a *paysan* **market** of regional products on Tuesday in May to November.

BONNIEUX

The appeal of this unspoilt village lies in its ancient grey-stone houses, its steps and its cobbled alleys clinging to vertiginous slopes. The spire of the 12th-century church rises above roofs of weathered tiles and is echoed by the pointed tops of cypress trees. From the highest points the views across the northern Lubéron are stunning. On the main street is a little **Musée de la Boulangerie** in an old bakery (*closed:* January and February, Tuesday in summer, Saturday and Sunday in the low season).

Accommodation

The **Hostellerie du Prieuré** (tel: 90 75 80 78), set in a serene, medieval priory at the foot of the village, is a beautiful building with stylish Provençal decor, a leafy garden (where meals are served) and some rooms at moderate prices.
L'Aiguebrun (tel: 90 74 04 14) is a gracious stone house secluded in a wooded combe east of Bonnieux; it enjoys total tranquillity and has the air of an aristocratic farmhouse. The rooms are quite expensive, but the restaurant has a good-value menu.

◆
BUOUX

Buoux consists of a handful of grey-stone houses scattered over the windswept hillside, surrounded by grassy pastures and lavender beds where only the sound of goat bells or crowing cocks breaks the peace. High on a craggy crest nearby is **Fort de Buoux**, set above a dramatic gorge; a 15-

The perched village of Bonnieux

minute walk uphill will bring you to the abandoned ruins of this ancient village and the remains of its medieval fort.

Accommodation

La Grande Bastide (tel: 90 74 29 10) is a big old farmhouse with attractively simple rooms at very reasonable rates.

Eating Out

Auberge de la Loube offers Provençal dishes at moderate prices (closed Thursday).

◆◆
LACOSTE

Here you will find an engaging knot of tiny cobbled streets and medieval houses, perched on a steep hill crowned by the imposing ruins of a **château**, once home to the Marquis de Sade. Lacoste is a remarkably quiet and unspoilt village, with lots of character – along the alleys you will come across a delicate campanile on Romanesque pillars, ancient archways and walls smothered in creepers or pots of bright flowers. There are splendid views of the wooded hillsides and vineyards, especially from around the castle. Just southwest, the part-ruined 12th-century **Abbaye St-Hilaire** is a peaceful spot.

Accommodation
Relais du Procureur (tel: 90 75 82 28) offers rooms in a lovely 17th-century stone mansion, with a pool in the inner courtyard, but is expensive.

Eating Out
Le Simiane serves a good choice of regional specialities at moderate prices (closed Wednesday and Thursday lunch).

LOURMARIN
This sizeable and very picturesque village lies in a combe; its narrow medieval streets are lined with honey-stone and pink or cream stucco houses, adorned with wrought-iron lamps and numerous pretty plants. The Renaissance **château** is a fine fortified mansion set in gardens, with an exquisite arcaded courtyard and impressive interiors (*closed:* Tuesday November to March, mornings October to June). The château also serves as an arts centre, regularly hosting concerts and exhibitions.

Vineyard near Ménerbes

Accommodation

The **Hostellerie du Paradou** (tel: 90 68 04 05) is a basic and very cheap *Logis* hotel with a shady dining terrace. The **Hôtel de Guilles**, Route de Vaugines (tel: 90 68 30 55) is a quiet farmhouse, with gardens, pool and moderate to expensive rooms, surrounded by vines and olives.

La Chaumière, Place du Portail, Lauris (tel: 90 08 20 25), is a creeper-clad building in a pretty village to the southwest; it is tastefully elegant, with wonderful views from the terraces – moderate to expensive.

Eating Out

La Fenière, Rue du Grand-Pré, is an intimate restaurant in a refurbished barn, serving tasty Provençal cuisine with good-value and more expensive menus (closed Sunday dinner and Monday).

◆
MENERBES

Ménerbes is another delightful perched village, clustered below a promontory with a medieval citadel (now a private residence). Many spots offer marvellous views, such as from the 14th-century church, or from opposite the traditional stone *lavoir* (where a few inhabitants still wash their clothes) at the bottom of the village. The old houses have been stylishly manicured into desirable homes with beautifully tended gardens and terraces. The grocer's shop is stocked with delicacies fit for refined Parisian palates. This is Peter Mayle territory, and his books (*A Year in Provence* and *Toujours Provence*) have attracted many new visitors. The **Massif des Cèdres**, to the south, is one of the best areas for walking.

Accommodation

Le Roy Soleil, Route des Beaumettes (tel: 90 72 25 61), lies below the village in a peaceful 17th-century stone farmhouse with smart rustic decor and a pool in the pretty gardens – expensive.

◆
OPPEDE-LE-VIEUX

This romantic medieval village has a quirky, crumbling charm. It is still semi-deserted, with many tumbledown, lichen-mottled stone buildings, and wild flowers growing between the broken cobbles. Its ancient ambience has attracted artists who have restored some of the 16th-century houses around the main square outside the ramparts.

The little **Musée Lagetus** has an exhibition varying from fossils to astronomy (*closed:* February). There is just one shop, selling crafts – and offering rooms. This is a gloriously atmospheric place for wandering around or just sitting at the café and soaking up the scenery.

THE PLATEAU DE VAUCLUSE

The central part of the *département* of Vaucluse consists of the high Plateau de Vaucluse which is separated from the Lubéron by the fertile Coulon valley. The plateau rises to similar heights as the

PLATEAU DE VAUCLUSE

Fontaine-de-Vaucluse

Lubéron, with rocky, scrubby hillsides densely covered in pine, oak and olive trees – wafting wonderful scents. The pale limestone of the plateau is cut by gorges and caves; underground rivers emerge as springs, notably at the famous Fontaine-de-Vaucluse. Ochre, a coloured soil used for making paint and dye pigments, is mined in parts of the plateau, especially towards the southeast around Rustrel Colorado, where there are cliffs and pinnacles of myriad radiant hues, from golden through coral to maroon.

Towards the north the plateau is more desolate and sparsely inhabited, but the southern slopes boast several picturesque *villages perchés* (perched villages), rising above the cultivated valleys. As everywhere, this countryside is suffused with a sense of history, and there are many evocative old buildings – from the superb abbey at Sénanque to primitive drystone *bories* (shepherds' huts) near Gordes.

FONTAINE-DE-VAUCLUSE

This village nestles at the foot of soaring cliffs and verdant slopes, below the mysterious source of the river Sorgue. A barricade of sheer rocky crags rises behind the spring, where the emerald-green water gushes from underground (except in late summer when it is reduced to a trickle). From here it tumbles down the gorge through the village where several cafés and hotels around the leafy central square have terraces over the river – the constant splash of running water is very soothing. Fontaine's other claim to fame is that the 14th-century poet Pétrarch lived here for a while; inspired by the wild beauty of the surroundings, he poured out poetry to Laura, the object of his unrequited love. The **Musée Pétrarque** has fine old editions of his work (*open:* weekends only in the low season; *closed:* Tuesday in summer). The **Moulin Vallis Clausa** displays various old methods of paper making, since the waters here once supplied several paper mills. **Le Monde Souterrain de Norbert Casteret** is concerned with the wonders of cave exploration and the history of the spring (*closed:* mid November to January, Monday and Tuesday in the low season).

Accommodation
Le Château, Quartier Petite Place (tel: 90 20 31 54), is a pleasant old building with a dining terrace over the river, offering very cheap rooms.

The rocky heights of Gordes

◆◆◆
GORDES ✓

Terraces of honey-stone houses cling to the sheer rocky slopes of this spectacular *village perché* dominated by its Renaissance château. Gordes is one of the most photographed villages in Provence – so sure of its high-ranking popularity that it boasts several upmarket hotels and a choice of smart art and craft shops. The impressive 12th and 16th-century château houses the **Musée Didactique Vasarely**, dedicated to the colourful geometric art of the Hungarian-born artist, Victor Vasarely; the museum also has a shop selling prints, tapestries and books (*closed:* Tuesday except July and August).
Just southwest of Gordes is the

Village des Bories, a group of beehive-shaped dry-stone buildings which are 200 to 500 years old (though examples elsewhere date back to neolithic times). The village now serves as a folk museum of rural life (*open:* daily).
To the south is the **Musée du Vitrail**, showing the history of stained glass; next to it is the **Moulin des Bouillons**, a 16th-century oil mill turned into a museum, with a huge wooden olive press (*both closed:* January, and Tuesday except in June to September).

Accommodation
Both these hotels are in a quiet rural setting east of Gordes. **La Ferme de la Huppe** (tel: 90 72

12 25) is a wonderful, rambling old farm with charming rooms around the courtyard and a pool in pretty gardens – quite expensive, but the menu is very good value. The **Auberge de Carcarille** (tel: 90 72 02 63) is a traditional stone *Logis* with a dining terrace and pool and reasonably priced rooms.

Eating Out

Le Mas Tourteron is a sophisticated and expensive restaurant just south of Gordes, in a lovely old house with a shady courtyard garden (closed Sunday dinner and Monday out of season). In an attractive village to the southwest, **Le Bistrot à Michel**, Cabrières d'Avignon, is a simple, friendly restaurant serving inventive dishes at moderate prices (closed Tuesday, plus Monday from September to June).

ROUSSILLON

This exceptionally pretty village is perched precariously on dramatic cliffs, layered in many glowing shades of gold, pink, rust and magenta – for this is an ochre-mining area. Its equally colourful houses are clustered on steep slopes, the russet and terracotta set off by contrasting blue shutters and green plants, against a backdrop of verdant hills with the azure sky above. Narrow streets and steps wind up past artisan shops and galleries, to a little square with café tables shaded by jolly red and white parasols. At the top of the hill, by the church, is a viewing platform offering magnificent panoramas. From the bottom of the village a path leads down to the disused ochre quarries.

Accommodation

The **Résidence des Ocres** (tel: 90 05 60 50), below the village, is a simple, old-fashioned *Logis* with a shady courtyard and rooms at reasonable rates. The **Mas de Garrigon** (tel: 90 05 63 22), set in peaceful woods just northeast, is full of rustic character, with a big fireplace, inviting armchairs, shelves of books and a pool. The rooms are expensive, but the rustic restaurant offers a good-value menu.

◆◆◆

SENANQUE, ABBAYE DE

Tucked into a tranquil, unspoilt valley, this beautiful 12th-century Cistercian abbey seems to blend harmoniously into its surroundings – with wooded, rocky slopes rising each side, and lavender fields in front. The pure lines of the weathered but well-preserved stone buildings, and its stark interior simplicity, give it a timeless serenity. Around the graceful cloisters are set the church and spacious living quarters. A group of monks has returned to live here, and a little shop sells the items which they make to support themselves. Along the road that winds through rugged countryside to Gordes, just south of the abbey, a superb panorama of the Lubéron unfolds before you. *Open:* daily 10.00–12.00 and 14.00–18.00 hrs, but to 17.00 hrs October to March. *Closed:* 10.00–12.00 hrs on Sunday and major religious holidays.

NORTH VAUCLUSE

Most views in the northern part of Vaucluse are dominated by the big, bold bulk of Mont Ventoux (6,263 feet/1,909m). The mountain is aptly named since its bare peak is swept by fierce winds. The summit, reached by driving up from the old village of Malaucène, is of a barren desert of pale pebbles rising above dense woods, which makes the peak look permanently snow-capped. Needless to say, Mont Ventoux offers breathtaking panoramas – when it is not enveloped in a halo of cloud. Another way to reach the top is to climb the steep footpath up the northeast face from **Brantes**, a little huddle of houses cascading down vertiginous slopes, just across the Toulourenc valley. There are gentler routes from the south and west. Apart from hiking, Ventoux is also popular for cycling and, in winter, skiing.

Southeast of Mont Ventoux, the spectacular Gorges de la Nesque cuts through the northern end of the Plateau de Vaucluse. A road winds tortuously along the cliff faces and crags of this precipitous gorge – with dizzying drops over 1,000 feet (300m) in places, and views of rugged mountains and deep, tree-clad valleys as far as the eye can see. Where the Nesque valley opens out to the east there are fragrant fields of lavender and mountain pastures.

Just to the west of Mont Ventoux lie the Dentelles de Montmirail, a serrated ridge of jagged limestone pinnacles, whose delicate outline against the sky gives them their name – *dentelle* means lace. The lower slopes to the west are fringed with well-known wine villages – lots of wine-tasting is advertised here. As a whole, this part of Provence has yet to gain the cachet of southern areas, so it is easier to find unspoilt spots and authentic rustic villages.

◆

LE BARROUX

This delightful village, set on a wooded hill southwest of Mont Ventoux, has an impressive medieval château (*Open:* July and August) perched on its rocky summit. Old stone houses, embellished with flowers and greenery, climb the steep streets around it, and there are marvellous views of

The village of Brantes

Ventoux and the Dentelles from the castle terrace.

Accommodation
Les Géraniums (tel: 90 62 41 08) is a simple, homely and low-priced *Logis* hotel on the edge of the village, with a quiet leafy garden and fine views from the dining terrace. In the tranquil hill village of Crillon-le-Brave, just southeast of here, is the **Hostellerie Crillon-le-Brave** (tel: 90 65 61 61), a beautiful old building with stylish Provençal decor, pretty gardens, a pool and great views – but very expensive.

GIGONDAS
Gigondas is a charming, unspoilt village with real local character, clustered on a hillside below the jagged peaks of the Dentelles de Montmirail. Its wine is reputed to be the best in the area – the wines of 50 or so different local vineyards can be sampled at the **Caveau de Gigondas** on the main square. The neighbouring tourist office can give advice on visiting individual *domaines*, and also walking or climbing in the area.

Accommodation
The following all have some rooms at reasonable rates. **Les Florets** (tel: 90 65 85 01) is a traditional *Logis* peacefully secluded in pine woods high on the slopes above Gigondas. **Château du Martinet**, Violès (tel: 90 70 94 98), is a grand 19th-century mansion on the main road to Vaison-la-Romaine, with a pool. Just southwest of here, **Mas de Bouvau**, Violès (tel: 90 70 94 08), is an attractive farmhouse with a garden.

Eating Out
L'Oustalet, Place du Portail, is an appealing restaurant on the main square, offering local cuisine and a low-priced menu (closed Tuesday).

SAULT
This small town, set in a commanding position on a rocky spur, is a good base for exploring the Gorges de la Nesque. The town itself consists of terraces of tall houses clinging to a cliff face, with superb views over mountains and the heady lavender fields. In the old quarter is a Romanesque church and municipal museum showing archaeological items and local paintings (*open:* July to August, Monday, Wednesday and Saturday only). Across the valley to the west is the tiny unspoilt village of **Monieux**, clustered on a sheer rocky slope, with the remains of a medieval watchtower above. Along the Gorges de la Nesque further west, look out for the **Rocher du Cire**, a crag rising to 650 feet (200m), where generations of wild bees have deposited their wax.

Eating Out
Les Lavandes, in Monieux, is a simple rustic inn, with a shady terrace, and low-priced menu (closed January).

SEGURET
Séguret, the most charming of the wine villages of the Dentelles de Montmirail,

snuggles against a steep hillside, the stone of the buildings suffused with the honey colour of the natural rocks. Through a medieval gateway are cobbled alleys lined with quaint houses leaning with age, and a pretty little square with a 14th-century clock-tower and fountain. There are some artisan shops and wine-tasting *caves* along the alleyways that zig-zag past leafy corners up to the old church, whose terrace gives stunning panoramas of the Rhône valley.

Nearby

Other appealing villages around the Dentelles include **Beaumes-de-Venise** to the south (renowned for its sweet muscat wine, and with a Romanesque chapel nearby), **Vacqueyras** to the northwest (offering wine-tasting in an old castle), **Sablet** and **Rasteau** (with a wine museum). Huddled high on the steep, rocky slopes of the wilder eastern side, nearer Ventoux, are tiny unspoilt villages such as **La Roque Alric**, **Lafare** and **Suzette**.

Accommodation

La Table du Comtat (tel: 90 46 91 49) is a *Logis* perched at the top of the village, converted from a 15th-century hospice, with superb views – on the expensive side.

Eating Out

Le Mesclun is a restaurant in an old stone house where you can sit and enjoy the views while eating tasty local cuisine at moderate prices.

Roman remains, Vaison-la-Romaine

◆◆◆
VAISON-LA-ROMAINE ✔

This appealing town, to the north of the Dentelles de Montmirail, is an animated and popular place with many attractions. The medieval quarter is clustered on a steep hill, crowned by a castle – once the site of a Celtic settlement called *Voconces*. Beneath it flows the River Ouvèze, spanned by a fine single-arched Roman bridge which joins it to the 'new' part of town (dating from the 18th century) where there are extensive Roman remains.

Two excavated areas – lying either side of the tourist office in Place du Chanoine-Sautel – clearly show the layout of the Roman town and the comfortable lifestyle of the citizens. The **Vestiges de Puymin** include the remains of houses, a colonnaded walkway and the theatre (which is used during the summer festival). There is also a **museum** here displaying many interesting statues, pots, jewellery, mirrors and tools. The **Fouilles de la**

NORTH VAUCLUSE

Villasse include remains of houses (some with mosaics), an arcaded shopping street, baths and a garden. Towards the edge of town, on the same side of the river, is the Romanesque **Cathédrale Notre-Dame-de-Nazareth**: Roman columns support the arcade around the 6th-century apse, and the tranquil medieval cloister has a collection of archaeological fragments. Past a tree-lined square with pavement cafés, and over the Roman bridge, the narrow cobbled streets of the medieval **Haute Ville** climb steeply. They are lined with lovely old stone houses adorned with plants and flowers, punctuated by little squares with pretty fountains, and an ancient belfry with an archway over the street. At the top of the hill are the ruins of a 12th-century **château**, once the country seat of the Counts of Toulouse – it is worth climbing up to this rocky summit for splendid views over the town to the hills beyond.

This old part of the town was deserted in the 18th century, in favour of the flatter land on the opposite river bank, but it has now been revived and there are several small artisan shops along the peaceful, picturesque streets. The newer part of town also has a variety of interesting shops selling Provençal specialities and arts and crafts – especially along **Grande Rue** (running from the Roman bridge towards the Roman sites). This is an important regional centre, and Vaison's Tuesday **market** has an enticing array of local produce.

Nearby
There are many pretty villages in the vicinity, including the dramatically perched **Crestet**, as well as **Faucon** and **Buisson** to the south.

Accommodation
Le Beffroi, Rue de l'Evêché (tel: 90 36 04 71), is a 16th-century residence at the heart of Vaison's medieval town, with a traditional ambience and lovely views from the terraced gardens – room prices range from quite reasonable to expensive. **Les Auric** (tel: 90 36 03 15) is an old house just west of Vaison, very pleasant with its bare stone and simple wooden furniture, offering rooms at reasonable prices and a pool.

The medieval Haute Ville above Vaison-la-Romaine

WEST BOUCHES-DU-RHONE

This historically important area centres on the colourful old town of Arles – once the capital of Roman Provence. It lies at the point where the Rhône splits into two arms to enclose the Camargue. Northeast of Arles, the chalky crags of the Chaîne des Alpilles jut abruptly from the valley plains; the bare, jagged rocks along the top, rising to 1,270 feet (387m) at La Caume, look like the crest of a wave and give way to scrubby pine woods, olive groves and vineyards on the lower slopes. This rugged ridge divides the two plains of La Petite Crau in the north from La Grande Crau to the south. The flat land of the Petite Crau is green and richly cultivated. The fields are lined with poplar and cypress trees planted to serve as windbreaks against the force of the mistral winds. The Grande Crau consists of a vast expanse of pebbles, worn smooth by the waters of the Durance which once flowed across this ancient delta directly into the sea. Some parts are irrigated by canals (there are rice fields near Arles) while the arid areas are given over to olive trees or winter pasture for sheep. Close to the Rhône, in the north-westernmost corner of the *département*, the choppy hills of La Montagnette rise to 540 feet (165m). The pale rocks of these hills are covered in fragrant scrub and fringed by pine woods, almond orchards and olive groves and vines. The ruined fortress perched on a hill by the quaint medieval village of Boulbon – with views of the river – is a remnant of the historic rivalry between France and Provence. This can also be seen in impressive proportions at Tarascon, where a mighty château stands by the Rhône glaring across at Beaucaire's castle on the opposite bank.

ARLES ✓

Most of this large but compact town is set on the east bank of the Grand Rhône, which glides gently around the northwest side of the old quarter. The centre boasts some superb monuments, bearing witness to its glorious past: *Arelate* became the capital of late Roman Gaul and was an important religious centre in the Middle Ages. As the gateway to the Camargue, Arles has many strong connections with this legendary land of *gardians* (cowboys) and gypsies. Van Gogh did much to make Arles famous – lovers of his paintings will recognise many scenes from the area. The main promenading street is the wide plane-lined **Boulevard des Lices**, running along the southern edge of the old town. There are several terraced cafés here, where you can sit and watch the world go by. **Rue Jean-Jaurès** and its continuation, **Rue Hôtel de Ville**, form the main north/south axis through the old town, at the centre of which is the **Place de la République**, bordered by some fine old buildings such as the beautiful church of St-Trophime.

Further into the maze of narrow streets is the **Place du Forum,** a shady square with lots of lively open-air cafés. To the east is the splendid Roman **Arènes** (Ampitheatre), while nearby, to the southwest, is the Roman **Théâtre** lying by the west edge of the cool, green **Jardin d'Eté** (Summer Garden).

Parts of the ancient ramparts can be seen nearby, around the eastern corner of the old town, along with remnants of a Roman aqueduct. To the north are further remains of the ramparts, and across the river lie the vestiges of a Roman bridge. Peaceful walks along the riverside *quais* (embankments) are especially appealing when the sun sets with a rosy glow over the pantiled roofs of the old town and the ever-flowing Grand Rhône.

Most of the main museums and monuments in Arles can be visited on a global entrance ticket which can be purchased at the tourist office (on Boulevard des Lices) or at any participating monument.

LES ALYSCAMPS
Avenue des Alyscamps
All that remains of this renowned Roman and medieval burial ground is a plane-lined avenue with a few sarcophagi and carved monuments – many others were given away as municipal gifts and some now reside in museums. At one end is the 12th-century Romanesque church of St-Honorat. This once-splendid site is still evocatively serene and its mood was caught on canvas by Van Gogh and Gauguin.

Open: November to February, daily 09.00– 12.00 and 14.00–16.30hrs; March and October, daily 09.00–12.30 and 14.00– 18.00hrs, April to 18.30hrs; May to 19.00hrs; June to September, daily 08.30–19.00hrs.

ARENES
Rond-Point des Arènes
The magnificent amphitheatre is the most impressive of Arles' Roman monuments. Two of the three original tiers of arches survive and it is still used as a venue for various events, including weekly bullfights. In the Middle Ages it was turned into a fortress, and three medieval towers remain – there are good views from the tower over the entrance.

Open: November to February, daily 09.00–12.00 and 14.00–16.30hrs; March and October, daily 09.00–12.30 and 14.00– 18.00hrs, April to 18.30hrs; May to 19.00hrs; June to September, daily 08.30–19.00hrs.

EGLISE ST-TROPHIME
Place de la République and Rue du Cloître
This gem among Provençal churches was first built in the 9th century though its most notable features date from the later in the Middle Ages. The wonderful 12th-century doorway has elaborately vivid carvings in the Provençal Romanesque tradition. The elegant cloister is quite exceptional – the north and east

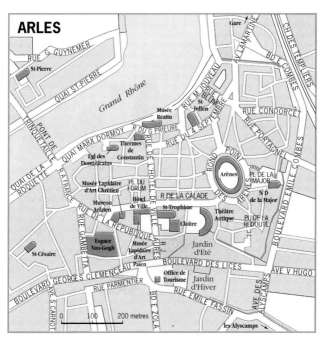

ARLES

galleries are Romanesque, while the south and west are in Gothic style. They are richly sculpted and surround tranquil gardens, with a good view of the fine Italianate tower.
Open: January, daily 10.00–12.00 and 14.00–16.30hrs; February, daily 10.00–12.30 and 14.00–19.00hrs; March to May, daily 09.30–12.30 and 14.00–19.00hrs; June to September, daily 09.00–19.00hrs; October, daily 09.30–12.30 and 14.00–18.00hrs; November 09.30–12.00 and 14.00–16.30hrs; December, daily 09.30–12.00 and 14.00–19.00hrs.

◆◆
MUSEE D'ART CHRETIEN
Rue Balze
This celebrated collection of 4th-century Christian sarcophagi, sculpted with biblical scenes, is housed in a 17th-century Jesuit chapel and is regarded as one of the best displays of its kind. Stairs lead down to the underground galleries of the Roman cryptoporticus, built as a granary beneath the forum.
Open: November to February, daily 09.00–12.00 and 14.00–16.30hrs; March and October, daily 09.00–12.30 and 14.00–18.00hrs; April to September to 19.00hrs.

The Arènes in Arles

◆
MUSEE LAPIDAIRE D'ART PAIEN
Place de la République
Yet more ancient sculpted stones, in this case mainly Greek and Roman, shown in the 17th-century Gothic church of Ste-Anne. They include some lovely mosaics and sculptures, plus a cast of the famous *Venus of Arles* (the original is in the Louvre).
Open: November to February, daily 09.00–12.00 and 14.00–16.30hrs; March and October, daily 09.00–12.30 and 14.00–18.00hrs; April to 18.30hrs; May to September to 19.00hrs.

◆◆
MUSEE REATTU
Rue du Grand Prieuré
This splendid 15th-century priory houses a varied art collection, including works by the local painter, Jacques Réattu, and other members of the 18th-century Provençal school. Best of all, though, are the paintings by Gauguin, Dufy, Vasarely and Picasso.
Open: November to January, daily 10.00–12.30 and 14.00–17.00hrs; February to April to 19.00hrs; May, daily 09.30–12.30 and 14.00–19.00hrs; June to September from 09.00hrs; October, daily 10.00–12.30 and 14.00–18.00hrs.

◆◆
MUSEON ARLATEN
Rue de la République
Literary hero Frédéric Mistral – who worked to promote Provençal language and culture – set up this ethnographic museum in a fine 16th-century *hôtel,* using the Nobel Prize

money he won in 1904. The Museon depicts every aspect of Provençal life, history and folklore through entertaining displays and a rich collection of costumes.
Open: October to May, 09.00–12.00 and 14.00–17.00hrs; June and September to 18.00hrs; July and August to 19.00hrs. *Closed:* Monday from October to May.

◆

THEATRE ANTIQUE
Rue de la Calade
Some imagination is needed to conjure up the appearance of the original Roman edifice built in the late 1st century BC, but enough remains for it to be used to stage events during the city's July Festival (see **Special Events** page 56).
Open: November to February, daily 09.00–12.00 and 14.00–16.30hrs; March and October, daily 09.00–12.30 and 14.00–18.00hrs; April to 18.30hrs; May to 19.00hrs; June to September, daily 08.30–19.00hrs.

◆

THERMES DE CONSTANTIN
Rue D Maïsto
The ruins of these Roman baths are all that remains of an impressive imperial palace built by the Emperor Constantine in the 4th century. Now pigeons roost in holes along the pink and grey walls.
Open: November to February, daily 09.00–12.00 and 14.00–16.30hrs; March and October, daily 09.00–12.30 and 14.00–18.00hrs; April to 18.30hrs; May to September to 19.00hrs.

Accommodation
There is a good range of hotels in town, with some quieter alternatives (and campsites) in the surrounding countryside.

In the Old Town
At the top end of the range is the expensive **Jules César**, Boulevard des Lices (tel: 90 93 43 20), a smart and spacious hotel with pool and garden set in a 17th-century convent with a colonnaded portico. The **Nord-Pinus**, 14 Place du Forum (tel: 90 93 44 44), is a splendid old hotel decorated with great style and panache, including beautiful antiques and souvenirs of the bullfighting stars who stay here.
Starting at slightly more moderate prices, the **Arlatan**, 26 Rue du Sauvage (tel: 90 93 56 66), is an old mansion with much charm and character, tucked away in a quiet corner. The **Forum**, 10 Place du Forum (tel: 90 93 48 95), is modern, with a pool and some rooms at quite reasonable rates.
Hotels with low-priced rooms include the simple and old-fashioned **Calendal**, 22 Place Pomme (tel: 90 96 11 89), between the Arènes and Théâtre. **Le Cloître**, 18 Rue du Cloître (tel: 90 96 29 50), is similar in style, with some rooms looking over the St-Trophime cloister. The **Musée**, 11 Rue du Grand Prieuré (tel: 90 93 88 88), facing the Musée Réattu, is also simple, traditional and very pleasant.

In the Surroundings
Mas de la Chapelle, Petite Route de Tarascon (tel: 90 93 23 15), in the countryside just north

of Arles, is a beautiful secluded 16th-century farmhouse and chapel, with elegant rustic decor, delightful shady gardens and two pools – rooms are on the expensive side. **Auberge La Fenière**, Raphèle-les-Arles (tel: 90 98 47 44), in a very peaceful setting 3 miles (5km) east of Arles, is an old-fashioned beamed farmhouse – room prices range from quite reasonable to quite expensive.

Eating Out

The old town has a wide choice of restaurants, including terraced café/brasseries on avenues such as the Boulevard des Lices and squares such as the Place du Forum. Restaurants offering moderately priced and more expensive set menus include **Lou Marquès**, at the Jules César hotel (see above), which has a lovely garden for formal dining and serves local specialities, **L'Olivier**, 1 bis Rue Réattu, in an old house hidden away in an alley, with a refined ambience, an attractive

Place de la République, Arles

courtyard and an imaginative menu (closed Sunday and Monday lunch) and Le **Vaccarès**, Place du Forum (entrance Rue Favorin), agreeably smart and rustic with a balcony overlooking the square, serving delicious regional cuisine (closed Sunday dinner and Monday). For a low-priced menu try **Hostellerie des Arènes**, 62 Rue du Refuge, a typical bistro opposite the ampitheatre, with pavement tables and an upstairs veranda, offering traditional family cooking (closed Tuesday dinner and Wednesday in the low season).

BOUCHES-DU-RHONE

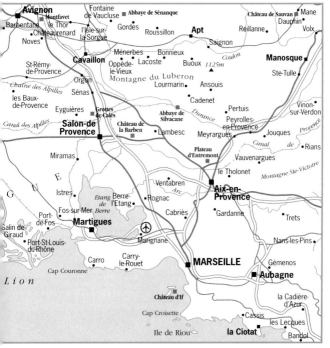

Shopping

There are some chic (and expensive) clothes and shoe boutiques around Rue Hôtel de Ville – where you will also find a variety of other good shops to tempt the eye and purse. Near the Arènes and Musée Réattu are some interesting antique and bric-a-brac shops. You will often see locals wearing traditional dress; and the distinctive printed fabrics, as well as items made from them, can be bought in **Souleiado**, 4 Boulevard des Lices, and nearby **Les Olivades**, 2 Rue J-Jaurès. Lots of shops in the old town sell typical local specialities, including lavender water, soap, dried flowers, herbs, honey, wine and pottery; a pretty selection of such items is sold at **La Boutigo**, 24 Boulevard des Lices. Beautifully hand-carved wooden items can be bought at **L'Art du Bois**, 29 Rue des Porcelets. A good choice of books, including some lovely ones on Provence, can be found at **Le Méjan**, 23 Quai Marx Dormoy, which also sells records and tapes, and has a restaurant and cinema.

A big and colourful **market** takes place every Saturday along Boulevard des Lices, Boulevard G Clemenceau and adjoining streets, with a stunning array of local produce.

There is also a **flea market** every Saturday and on the first Wednesday of the month.

Nightlife

Arles has very little nightlife, apart from the cafés. The cinema at **Le Méjan**, 23 Quai Marx Dormay, shows interesting films. The mature crowd go to dance at **Le Krystal**, near Raphèle-lès-Arles (east of Arles). Most of the trendy set go to St-Rémy, where **Club de la Haute Galine**, Quartier de la Galine, is very popular; also in St-Rémy is **Le News**, Place de la République, and **La Forge des Trinitaires**, Avenue de la Libération (reggae and African music, closed in summer). Another popular disco is **Le Plantation**, near L'Albaron (in the Camargue). These clubs open weekends only – ask at the tourist office on Boulevard des Lices for details.

Special Events

The Saturday afternoon bullfights in the Arènes are a popular and dramatic spectacle – in the Provençal version the aim is not to kill the bull but to show agility and daring by snatching ribbons from the animal's horns. Festivities include the **Easter Feria** (bullfighting), **La Fête des Gardians** (cattle-herding skills) on 1 May, the July festivals of photography and of music and drama, with the traditional **Fête d'Arles** in the first week, the **Peplum Film Festival** at the end of August and the **Prémices du Riz** (rice-harvest festival) in mid-September.

The Pont de Langlois by the banks of the Rhône in Arles

Cathédral d'Images, Les Baux

◆◆
BARBENTANE

This charming, sleepy hill town lies close to the confluence of the Rhône and the Durance. In the atmospheric medieval quarter, opposite the old church, is the **Maison des Chevaliers**, a Renaissance house with an arcaded gallery and turret. On top of the hill stands the 14th-century **Tour Angelic**. Outside the old quarter is a most elegant 17th-century mansion, the **Château de Barbentane**, an Italianate building with sumptuous marble floors, painted ceilings and delicate Louis XV and XVI furniture, surrounded by graceful gardens (*open:* daily July to September, Thursday to Tuesday from Easter to June and in October; Sunday only November to Easter).

Just south, the tropical gardens of **Provence Orchidées** are resplendent with orchids and live butterflies (*open:* daily).

◆◆◆
LES BAUX-DE-PROVENCE

Dramatically set high on a desolate rocky spur in the Alpilles, this legendary citadel blends into the bare cliffs on which it is perched – at night the twinkling lights of the village seem suspended in the sky. The notorious feudal lords of Les Baux, described as a 'race of eagles' by the Provençal poet, Mistral, were a ruthless lot – pushing people off the cliffs for fun. Les Baux was also celebrated for its troubadour courts of love. The stunningly impressive site, with marvellous bird's-eye views, throngs with visitors in the summer so it is best to visit early or late in the day if you can. The narrow cobbled streets of the village – lined with many beautiful Renaissance mansions – wind up to the so-called **Cité Morte** (Dead City) (*open:* 08.30–19.00 hrs in summer, to sunset in low season). Here the evocative ruined shells of the ancient town include an imposing medieval fortress standing on the cliff-top. The village has several museums. The **Musée d'Art Contemporain**, in the 16th-century Hôtel de Manville (also the tourist office), shows local paintings, sculptures and photographs (*open:* summer daily 08.30– 20.00hrs; winter daily 09.00–17.00hrs). The Fondation Louis Jou (*open:* daily, April to October), in another wonderful 16th-century *hôtel*, has some superb medieval and Renaissance books, plus prints and engravings (including work by

Goya). Other museums (*open: daily*) include: the **Musée Lapidaire** showing local history, the **Musée des Santons** with a display of local Nativity figures, the **Musée de l'Olivier** on the olives of Provence and the **Fondation Yves Brayer** showing the work of this local artist. At the north-west foot of the rocky outcrop, sheer cliffs and crags rise each side of the Val d'Enfer (Valley of Hell), scattered with green pines and scrub. Just outside Les Baux, in this suitably surreal setting, an old quarry has been turned into the **Cathédrale d'Images**, with spectacular slide and music shows projected around the caverns (*closed:* 12 November to early December and early January to February).

Accommodation
La Cabro d'Or (tel: 90 54 40 46), near the Val d'Enfer, is a sophisticated farmhouse hotel with a pool in lush gardens – expensive, but less so than its nearby sister hotel, the luxurious **L'Oustau de Baumanière** (tel: 90 54 33 07) which has a renowned restaurant. Below Les Baux's fortress, **Le Mas d'Aigret** (tel: 90 97 33 54) is a charming old farmhouse with a dining room carved out of the rocks, a pool and fine views – from quite expensive upwards.
In the valley just south-west, **La Benvengudo**, Vallon de L'Arcoule (tel: 90 54 32 54), is a creeper-clad farmhouse with traditional decor and peaceful gardens with a pool – moderate to expensive.
Two simple *Logis*, with pools

and rooms at reasonable rates are **La Ripaille**, Route des Baux, Fontvieille (tel: 90 97 73 15), a very pretty, quiet hotel south-west of Les Baux and **Les Magnanarelles**, Mausanne (tel: 90 54 30 25), a pleasant hotel in an attractive olive and wine village south of Les Baux.

Eating Out
The **Bérengère** is a tiny, genial restaurant at the top of the village, offering inventive local dishes and moderate to expensive menus (*closed:* Tuesday dinner, Wednesday and November). **La Riboto de Taven**, nestling below the rocks of the Val d'Enfer, is an elegant rustic restaurant with a shady terrace, serving classic cuisine at higher prices (closed Sunday dinner in low season, Monday and January to February).

FONTVIEILLE
The houses of this delightful village drip with creepers that complement the green colour of their shutters. The picturesque **Moulin de Alphonse Daudet** sits on a rocky hill on the southern outskirts, with views of the scented scrubby foothills of the Alpilles. The 19th-century novelist, Alphonse Daudet, was inspired to write his *Lettres de Mon Moulin* (*Letters from My Windmill*) by the stories that were told to him by the miller here. The mill now houses a tiny museum (*open:* daily but Sunday only in January). Southwest of Fontvieille lie the impressive but rather sombre

Ancient narrow streets in St-Rémy-de-Provence

Les Antiques, St-Rémy

Romanesque ruins of the fortified **Abbaye de Montmajour**, dating from the 12th and 17th centuries. The cloister has fine carvings, and there are wonderful views from the high watchtower (*open: daily except for holidays and major fêtes*).

Accommodation

In the old quarter, the **Auberge de la Régalido** (tel: 90 97 60 22) is a lovely former oil mill, tranquil and beautifully furnished with antiques but expensive. Two simple *Logis* in appealing old houses are the **Laetitia**, 21 Rue du Lion (tel: 90 97 72 14), with rustic character and very low prices, and the **Hostellerie de la Tour**, 31 Rue des Plumelets (tel: 90 97 72 21), on the outskirts, with rooms around the garden and pool, at low rates.

Eating Out

Le Patio, 117 Route du Nord, is a lively little restaurant with a flowery patio and local menu at moderate prices (closed Tuesday dinner, Wednesday and January).

◆◆◆
ST-REMY-DE-PROVENCE ✓

St Rémy has all the allure of a truly traditional Provençal town, lying at the foot of the rugged Alpilles, amid the gentle green countryside of La Petite Crau. St-Rémy is a market centre for flowers, fruit, vegetables and herbs as well as a favourite haunt of artists, past and present (notably Van Gogh) and an ideal base for touring the region. The town remains unspoilt yet has much quiet style and touches of sophistication. Shady boulevards lined with plane trees and a variety of pavement cafés surround the *vieille ville* (old town), a tangle of ancient narrow streets scattered with Renaissance mansions, leafy sun-dappled squares and splashing fountains.

By Place Favier are two museums in beautiful 15th and 16th-century *hôtels*: the **Musée des Alpilles** has interesting displays on the traditions, arts, crafts, folklore and people of the area (including Nostradamus, who was born here) and the **Musée Archéologique** shows Greek and Roman finds from Glanum (see below), south of St-Rémy (*both museums closed:* January to March).

On Rue Estrine is **Le Centre d'Art Van Gogh**, a grand 18th-century mansion with exhibitions of modern art; despite the name there are no original Van Gogh paintings here, but a video documents his life and work (*closed:* Monday). Van Gogh came here from Arles to convalesce for a year after his quarrel with Gauguin and the famous ear-cutting incident. He stayed at an asylum in an old monastery, **St-Paul-de-Mausole**, outside St-Rémy to the south. Its 12th-century Romanesque church, with a pretty tower and charming carved cloister, can be visited.

Below the rocky hills nearby, standing in isolated splendour on one side of the road, are **Les Antiques**, a part-ruined triumphal arch celebrating the Roman conquest of Marseilles and a well-preserved, elaborately sculpted mausoleum. Opposite lie the remains of the Graeco-Roman town of **Glanum**, built on the site of an earlier neolithic homestead (*open:* daily).

In the rural village of Maillane, a few miles northwest of St-Rémy, the **Museon Frédéric Mistral** is the old home of this Nobel prize-winning poet and champion of Provençal culture, preserved as it was at his death in 1914 (*closed:* Monday).

Accommodation and Eating Out

The **Hôtel des Antiques**, 15 Avenue Pasteur (tel: 90 92 03 02), is a 19th-century mansion with walled grounds full of trees, a conservatory terrace and pool – moderate to quite expensive. **La Reine Jeanne**, Boulevard Mirabeau (tel: 90 92 15 33), is a *Logis* with a pretty creeper-clad dining courtyard, rustic restaurant and comfortable rooms at reasonable rates. Two basic hotels in Boulevard Victor-Hugo

WEST BOUCHES-DU-RHONE

with rooms starting at very low prices are the **Hôtel des Arts** (tel: 90 92 08 50), with lots of pictures on the walls and a lively pavement café, and **De Provence** (tel: 90 92 06 27), a big, characterful old house with a lovely leafy garden.

In the peaceful, rocky foothills just southwest is the ultra-expensive **Domaine de Valmouriane** (tel: 90 92 44 62), a superb stone house with chic decor, pool, garden, excellent facilities and a good-value menu. In the countryside just west are two tranquil hotels secluded in wonderful wooded parks, both with pools: **Château des Alpilles** (tel: 90 92 03 33) is a gracious 19th-century mansion with opulent furnishings but expensive; **Château de Roussan** (tel: 90 92 11 63), an 18th-century mansion full of country character and antiques, is moderate to expensive. Near the enchanting hill village of Eygalières, southeast of St-Rémy, the **Mas du Pastre** (tel: 90 95 92 61) is a quiet old Provençal farmhouse decorated with freshness and simplicity; it has a pool and a self-catering apartment and room costs range from quite reasonable upwards.

Shopping

The **market** on Wednesday morning has wonderful displays of herbs, spices, aromatic plants, delicious foods and antiques. There are some good shops, including branches of **Souleiado** and **Les Olivades** in the old town. Craft, herbal and bric-a-brac shops are found in boulevards Victor-Hugo,

Gambetta and Mirabeau, and it is worth seeking out the **Herboristerie Provençal** on the northeastern outskirts.

Nightlife

Visitors come from afar for three of St-Rémy's trendy nightclubs, the **Club de la Haute Galine** (Quartier de la Galine), **Le News** (Pl de la République) and **Le Forge des Trinitaires** (Avenue de la Liberation – closed in summer).

TARASCON

The most striking feature of this typical Provençal town is the majestic, moated **Château du Roi René** lying by the side of the Rhône. This classic 15th-century fortress has massive cream stone walls, with graceful Gothic chambers inside – empty apart from some rich 17th-century tapestries (*open:* daily except for holidays). Good views from the battlements include the less intact but still impressive rival castle of **Beaucaire** across the Rhône (*closed:* Tuesday).

Close to the château entrance is the fine 12th-century Romanesque and 14th-century Gothic **Collégiale Ste-Marthe**; in the hushed crypt lies the tomb of Ste-Marthe who tamed the legendary monster La Tarasque – a ferocious beast with a lion's head and crocodile's tail. A colourful festival, decreed by King René in the 15th century, celebrates this legend during the last weekend of June.

The alleys of the old town have a crumbling aged appeal. They come to life on market day

(Tuesday), especially the arcaded medieval Rue des Halles, where the elegant 17th-century Hôtel de Ville is set. The **Musée Souleiado** has a reconstruction of a 19th-century Provençal home and a display of costumes (*closed:* Saturday and Sunday) plus a shop selling traditional fabrics. Art exhibitions are held in the pretty 16th-century **Cloître des Cordeliers** and, just north of the old town, the **Maison de Tartarin** has a little museum on the famous character created by the novelist, Alphonse Daudet (*both open:* daily).

In the pine-wooded valley of La Montagnette, to the northeast, is the **Abbaye St-Michel-de-Frigolet** (the name comes from the Provençal word for thyme, which perfumes the air), a tranquil working monastery; some of its Romanesque buildings can be visited, including the cloister (*open:* from 14.30hrs weekdays, 16.00hrs Sunday). You can also eat in the dining room, and buy souvenirs in the shop which sells the monks' own liqueur, honey and paintings.

Tarascon's Château du Roi René

THE CAMARGUE

THE CAMARGUE ✓

The famous white horses of the Camargue

This huge delta, embraced by the two arms of the river – the Grand Rhône to the east and the Petit Rhône to the west – has a unique and fascinating character. It consists of some 480 square miles (800 square km) of shimmering reed-fringed marshes, lagoons, mud-flats and long stretches of dunes and beaches. Where the land has been drained it is crisscrossed by canals and dikes and is used to grow crops such as rice. The local wine, called *vin des sables*, is produced from vines grown in sand to the west.

The Camargue countryside is flecked with many lovely wildflowers and dotted with lonely *mas* (farmhouses), sparkling white in the sun, or thatched *cabanes*, the traditional homes of the *gardians* (Camargue cowboys).

They can be seen riding white horses and herding the wild black bulls which are used for many spectacles in the area, including the bullfights in Arles; in the local version of the bullfight, known as *courses à la cocarde*, agile *razeteurs* (toreodors) snatch a red cockade from the bull's horns, rather than fighting the bull to the death as in Spanish-style *mise-à-mort* bullfights.

The famous white horses of the Camargue – which are born black or brown and only turn white after about four years – roam freely over the grassy marshland, just like the bulls. They are used to give rides to tourists; you will see plenty of horses lined up, with their big leather saddles, and signs offering *promenade à cheval* – especially along the coastal road from Stes-Maries to Arles.

Certain aspects of the Camargue are rather commercialised, but much is unspoilt. As a Parc Naturel Régional, its traditional ways of life and the wealth of wildlife are protected. The large lagoon of the Etang de Vaccarès, a nature reserve, is off-limits to ordinary visitors but there are nature trails nearby where you can see lots of wildlife – especially birds (field glasses are invaluable – see also the **Peace and Quiet** section). The Camargue appears at its most magical when the flamingos are seen across the lagoon in the reflected light of the setting sun.

Late spring or autumn are the best times to visit – for the festivals and flora as well as for the migrating birds. In the hot, humid summer, the dreaded mosquitoes are at their worst. Even so, the area is popular for its beaches; by walking along the coast you can find deserted spots (and a naturist zone east of Stes-Maries). Behind Plage de Piémanson, in the southeast, are saltpans and a lunar landscape of white salt hills, with a viewing platform near the salt town of Salin-de-Giraud.

◆◆
CENTRE D'INFORMATION DE GINES
Pont de Gau
This centre, north of Stes-Maries, provides an interesting introduction to the attractions of the Camargue through exhibitions and a video documentary.
Open: daily, but closed Friday October to March

◆◆
CENTRE D'INFORMATION DE RESERVE NATIONALE
La Capelière
Set on the east side of the Étang de Vaccarès, this is a good starting point for seeing the wildlife around the reserve, with interesting exhibitions and nature trail leaflets.
Closed: Sunday.

◆◆
CHATEAU D'AVIGNON
Lying 8 miles (13km) north of Stes-Maries, in verdant wooded grounds by the Petit Rhône, this imposing mansion was turned into a luxurious hunting lodge in the 19th century; the rich furnishings include antique tapestries, carved woodwork and fine paintings.
Open: daily April to September.

◆
MEJANES
This popular spot on the north-west side of the Étang de Vaccarès offers horse-riding, bull shows, *petit train* rides by the lake, barbecues, a café and a souvenir kiosk.

◆◆
MUSEE CAMARGUAIS
Housed in an old barn at the Mas du Pont de Rousty, north-east of L'Albaron, this museum has innovative displays showing the history, traditions, economy and lifestyles of the area.
Open: daily, but closed Tuesday October to March.

◆
MUSEE DE CIRE/AGRICOLE
North of Stes-Maries
Waxwork figures and local agricultural artefacts.
Open: daily April to September.

MUSEE TSIGANE
Pioch-Badet
Painted caravans showing gypsy traditions.
Open: daily.

LA PALISSADE
Set by the Grand Rhône just south-east of Salin, this has exhibitions to show the wildlife of the nearby lagoons, an herbarium, an aquarium and guided tours along the nature trails.
Open: daily but closed Saturday and Sunday from September to mid-June.

PARC ORNITHOLOGIQUE
Pont de Gau
This large area of marsh is laid out with trails designed to help visitors see birds in their natural habitat. There are informative pictures and maps at the entrance, and aviaries containing species that are difficult to see in the wild.
Open: daily.

LES SAINTES-MARIES-DE-LA-MER (STES-MARIES)
Stes-Maries is a busy seaside resort of little whitewashed houses, with the crenellated belfry of the ancient stone **church** rising above the tiled rooftops. The church was fortified to withstand Saracen raids in the 11th century.
In the crypt is a statue of Sara, patron saint of the gypsies. According to legend, Mary Magdalene, along with Mary Salomé (mother of the Apostles James and John), Mary Jacobé (the Virgin's sister) their servant Sara, Marthe and others, were driven out of Palestine and put in a boat without sails or oars. They eventually drifted to this spot, hence its name. Sara and two of the Marys settled here. Their relics were 'discovered' in the church in the 15th century and for centuries Stes-Maries has been a place of pilgrimage for gypsies from all over southern Europe. On the 24 and 25 May there is a wonderfully colourful festival: processions carry votive statues to the sea for a blessing by the bishop in a fishing boat, accompanied by *gardians* on horseback and many others in full costume, followed by flamenco music and bullfights in the arena by the seafront.
In summer the resort has a jolly, touristy atmosphere. The narrow streets of the old quarter and the seafront promenade are lined with souvenir shops and cafés. The **Musée Baroncelli**, in an old mansion near the church, includes local history, folklore and art (*closed:* Tuesday from October to May). A wide beach of greyish sand stretches all along the coast: quiet spots (and horse-riding) can be found to the west.
The town also has a lively little pleasure port, where boat tours of the Camargue and fishing trips are offered; jeep safaris also depart from here. The tourist office on the central seafront (Avenue Van Gogh) has details of excursions, which include visits to a *mas* to see *gardians* work the horses and bulls, and gypsy entertainment.

Les Saintes-Maries

Nearby

Just over the border of the Petit Rhône, 10 miles (16km) west of Arles, in atmospheric **St-Gilles**, the 12th-century **Abbatiale church** has superbly carved Romanesque doorways. To the southwest is the impressive fortified medieval town of **Aigues-Mortes**, from where St-Louis embarked on a crusade in the 13th century. The town is wonderfully preserved and there are fine views of the Camargue from the splendid **Constance Tower** on the ramparts.

Accommodation

The following are all peaceful hotels, located within 6 miles (4km) of Stes-Maries. **Mas des Rièges**, Route de Cacharel (tel: 90 47 85 07), offers simple comfort and a pool – rooms moderate to quite expensive. **Le Pont des Bannes**, Route d'Arles (tel: 90 97 81 09), a white *mas*-style building set by a stream and lagoon, has expensive rooms in thatched *cabanes* and a pool. **Pont de Gau**, Route d'Arles (tel: 90 97 81 53), is a pleasant, simple *Logis* by the Parc Ornithologique, with old-fashioned rustic appeal, at very reasonable rates.

Mas du Clarousset, Route de Cacharel (tel: 90 97 81 66), has wonderful views over the marshes and lagoons; a pool and expensive rooms with traditional Camarguais decor.

Lou Mas Du Juge, Pin-Fourcat (tel: 66 73 51 45), in verdant countryside by the Petit Rhône, is a working farm that takes guests; the 17th-century house is full of character and has a tremendous main room with beams, huge fireplace and magnificent old furnishings including a long wooden table where everyone eats together – expensive.

EAST AND CENTRAL BOUCHES-DU-RHONE

Of all the striking contrasts to be seen in Provence, one of the greatest is between the refined university town of Aix and the raffish port of Marseilles, just 15 miles (24km) apart. The nearby coastal area is densely populated, with extensive industrial developments around Marseilles and the Etang de Berre to the west. Even in the midst of the ugly refineries there is, however, one radiant gem of traditional charm: the fishing harbour of Martigues, set on canals joining the lake to the sea.

The countryside inland is beautifully unspoilt and scattered with timeless rural villages. The coast also boasts some dramatic scenery: high cliffs plunge to the iridescent Mediterranean sea, bordered by sandy beaches and backed by rocky, pine-wooded mountains. The steep slopes of the Massif de la Ste-Baume rise east of the market town of Aubagne, headquarters of the Foreign Legion, and more romantically associated with Marcel Pagnol, creator of *Jean de Florette*. Around Aix lie rugged hills, woods and areas of mellow, rolling farmland splashed with shades of russet and green – cultivated with almond groves, vineyards and other crops. The most evocative landmark is the marbled ridge of Montagne Ste-Victoire, immortalised by Cézanne. Wild, rocky hills stretch northwards, with densely wooded slopes along the wide, abundantly fertile valley of the Durance. West of Aix is the verdant Arc valley, another of Cézanne's favourite spots, where the impressive 19th-century Aqueduct de Roquefavour straddles a sheer gorge, near the pretty village perché of Ventabren. Further west, the flat plains and rocky ridges and outcrops around Salon have a rather stark, stony aspect with scented scrub, stunted pines and olive groves.

AIX-EN-PROVENCE

Aix has long been a prosperous cultural and intellectual centre. After the Romans conquered the Celto-Ligurian capital of *Oppidum d'Entremont*, located on a hill to the north, they founded a spa town here – *Aquae Sextiae* – which became a Roman administrative capital. Aix's medieval court, set up in the 12th century by the counts of Provence, reached an apogee of brilliance – renowned for its patronage of the arts and popular festivities – in the 15th century, under the much-loved King René d'Anjou. This regional capital was the seat of the local parliament until the French Revolution. Its architectural peak came in the 17th and 18th centuries, when deliberate urban planning transformed it into a city of harmonious post-Renaissance classical buildings.

The character of the old centre is beautifully preserved, and aristocratic mellow-stone mansions border the wide, main thoroughfare, **Cours**

EAST AND CENTRAL BOUCHES-DU-RHONE

Mirabeau (a promenade that replaced the medieval ramparts in the 17th century). It is shaded by a canopy of huge, stately plane trees and several fountains are set along its length – including La Rotonde, at the western end, facing the tourist office, and another with a statue of King René at the eastern end. The north side of Cours Mirabeau is lined with animated pavement cafés. This is where everyone goes to sit or stroll and watch the world go by. Like the town itself, the inhabitants of Aix seem supremely stylish; many are young because, apart from the venerable university (founded in 1409 and popular with foreign students) Aix has several colleges for art, music and dance. The city's devotion to culture reaches its height in July, with a major music festival. To the south of Cours Mirabeau lies the **Quartier Mazarin**, a model of well-planned 17th- and 18th-century architecture. There are many handsome honey-stone *hôtels* in the serene, ordered streets of this quiet district. The **Place Quatre Dauphins** has a pretty fountain and the elegant 13th century Gothic **Eglise-St-Jean-de-Malthe** lies on a square to the east

North of Cours Mirabeau, the narrow streets of **Vieil Aix** buzz with life. Here you will find busy shops and open-air cafés and more tranquil spots, such as the charming cobbled **Place d'Albertas**. At the heart of the old quarter is the splendid **Place de l'Hôtel de Ville**, with its 17th-century Italianate town hall (containing a collection of ancient books), the 18th-century corn exchange, which is now a post office, and the 16th-century Tour de l'Horloge, which has four rotating statues to show the seasons as well as a clock to show the time.

Off this square is the **Place Richelme**, host to a market every morning, and – via the clock tower archway – the spacious cobbled **Place des Cardeurs**. By another market square, Place des Prêcheurs, immediately to the east, you will find the 17th-century **Eglise Ste-Marie-Madeleine**, with a fine medieval triptych and a painting by Rubens.

The steeple of the **Cathédrale St-Sauveur** rises above the rooftops to the north. Not far off, in the northwest corner and close to the site of the original Roman baths, is the 18th-century **Thermes Sextius**; this offers spa cures and is set in a park which contains remains from the 14th-century ramparts.

View from Cézanne's house, Aix

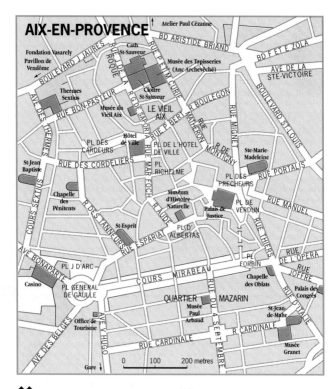

AIX-EN-PROVENCE

◆◆
ATELIER PAUL CEZANNE
9 Avenue Paul Cézanne
Even when he was living in
Paris, Cézanne often came
back to his home town. His
studio-house, set in a leafy
garden north of Vieil Aix, is
preserved exactly as it was
when he died in 1906 – with
his easel, books, drawings,
bottles, wine glass, pipe and
a simple, peaceful
atmosphere.
Open: Wednesday to Monday
10.00–12.00 and
14.30–18.00hrs (14.00–17.00hrs
in October to May).

◆◆
CATHEDRALE ST-SAUVEUR
Rue Gaston-de-Saporta
Aix's cathedral is built in a
wonderful mixture of styles. The
5th-century baptistry has
Roman columns supporting a
Renaissance cupola, and a total-
immersion pool. The original
12th-century church was
expanded in the 15th and 16th
centuries so both Romanesque
and Gothic can be seen in the
façade and nave. Of the façade
sculptures, only the Virgin is
original. There is also an
enchanting Romanesque
cloister. One of the cathedral's

art treasures is the 15th-century triptych, *Le Buisson Ardent* – with painted panels showing the Burning Bush and King René; another is the Renaissance carving of the central doors (both are kept locked so ask the custodian to open them). The fine Brussels tapestries were made in 1511 for Britain's Canterbury cathedral but sold at a bargain price to a priest from Aix during the Cromwellian period.
Open: daily except when services are being held.

FONDATION VASARELY
Avenue M Pagnol Jas-de-Bouffan
Vasarely, the Hungarian-born artist, designed this modern building on the western outskirts to house his own works, including colourful geometric paintings, tapestries and murals.
Open: 09.30–12.30 and 14.00–17.30 hrs. *Closed:* Tuesday in September to June.

MUSEE ARBAUD
2a Rue du 4 Septembre
This 18th-century mansion in the Quartier Mazarin has rooms lined with ancient leather-bound Provençal books, celebrated regional ceramics, paintings and historic artefacts.
Open: 14.00–17.00 hrs. *Closed:* Sunday.

MUSEE GRANET
Place St-Jean-de-Malte
This lovely 17th-century priory in the Quartier Mazarin, contains a wealth of art and archaeological treasures. They include a rare collection of Celto-Ligurian sculptures and paintings representing the major European schools from the 16th to the 19th century. Provençal artists are represented by Granet and Cézanne.
Open: 10.00–12.00 and 14.00–18.00 hrs.
Closed: Tuesday.

MUSEE DES TAPISSERIES
Place des Martyrs-de-la-Résistance
The grand 17th-century archbishop's palace, alongside the cathedral, has a display of magnificent 17th and 18th-century Beauvais tapestries, several showing scenes from *Don Quixote*. There is also a contemporary section.
Open: 10.00–12.00 and 14.00–18.00hrs.
Closed: Tuesday.

MUSEE DU VIEIL AIX
17 Rue Gaston-de-Saporta
In an impressive 17th-century *hôtel*, eclectic exhibits show the traditions, arts and history of the area, including a huge collection of *santons* – Provençal Christmas crib figures.
Open: mid April to September, Tuesday to Sunday 10.00–12.00 and 14.30–18.00 hrs; October to mid-April, Tuesday to Sunday 10.00–12.00 and 14.00 – 17.00hrs. *Closed:* Monday.

MUSEUM D'HISTOIRE NATURELLE
6 Rue Espariat
A fine series of rooms in one of Vieil Aix's most splendid 17th-

century *hôtels* are used to house a range of stuffed birds, insects and fossils plus some rare dinosaur eggs.
Open: 10.00–12.00 and 14.00–18.00hrs. *Closed:* Sunday morning.

◆◆
PAVILLON VENDOME
32 Rue Célony
This gracious 17th-century cardinal's country house, set in gardens just west of the Thermes Sextius, displays fine Provençal period furnishings and *objets d'art.*
Open: 10.00–12.00 and 14.00–17.00hrs; to 18.00hrs in summer. *Closed:* Tuesday.

Nearby
Cabriès is a classic perched village – set halfway between Aix and Marseille – with a **château** built for the counts of Provence between the 5th and the 13th centuries. It contains paintings by Edgar Mélik, who bought it in 1934 (*closed:* Tuesday).
To the southwest of Aix is **Montagne Ste-Victoire**, a rugged limestone ridge whose intricately sculpted slopes and changing moods were often painted by Cézanne. To the west, **Le Tholonet** is a peaceful village shaded by avenues of vast plane trees; you can walk northeast from the impressive dam, the **Barrage de Bimont**, where there are nature trails set among the picturesque woods and rocky gorges (the nearby Barrage Zola was designed by the father of Emile Zola, the famous writer and schoolfriend of Cézanne).
La Croix de Provence, on the crest of the mountain, offers stupendous panoramas. It can be reached by a steep climb up the sheer southern face or a longer hike up the gentler northern flanks, and a path continues along to the summit, **Pic des Mouches** (3,316 feet/ 1,011m). On the north side lies the pretty village of **Vauvenargues**; the mellow, red-shuttered château, standing on a spur, was Picasso's home and he is buried in the gardens (private). From here a narrow road snakes north through wild, wooded gorges to the appealing wine village of **Jouques**, near the Durance. Just north of Aix, the **Plateau d'Entremont** was the site of a Celto-Ligurian *oppidum*, a fortified hill town. Vestiges of the walls remain and there are good views of Aix (*closed:* Tuesday).

Accommodation
Aix has plenty of hotels but there is not a great choice if you are on a strict budget. Do not forget that there is a huge demand for hotel rooms at festival time in July and early August.

In the Centre
Among the expensive hotels are **Le Pigonnet**, 5 Avenue du Pigonnet (tel: 42 59 02 90), a charming old country house with a pool set in a tranquil wooded park just southwest of the centre, and **Des Augustins**, 3 Rue de la Masse (tel: 42 27 28 59), a serene and comfortable 12th-century convent off Cours Mirabeau, where antiques set off the medieval style of the building.

Hotels with moderately-priced rooms include the **Nègre-Coste**, 33 Cours Mirabeau (tel: 42 27 74 22), one of Aix's oldest hotels, with a suitably grand, old-fashioned ambience and, in contrast, **Des Quatre Dauphins**, 54 Rue R Alphéran (tel: 42 38 16 39), a pretty, intimate place in the Quartier Mazarin, with chic Provençal decor.

Rooms at reasonable rates can be found at **Le Manoir**, 8 Rue d'Entrecasteaux (tel: 42 26 27 20), a converted 14th-century cloister tucked away in a quiet corner of Vieil Aix. Slightly cheaper is **De France**, 63 Rue Espariat (tel: 42 27 90 15), a simple, old-fashioned hotel on a busy street in Vieil Aix.

In the Surroundings
Expensive hotels include the **Château de la Pioline**, Les Milles (tel: 42 20 07 81), a beautiful, aristocratic mansion, set by the river Arc southwest of Aix, with light, spacious rooms, elegant antique decor and a pool; and **Le Mas**

The bounty of Provence

d'Entremont, Montée d'Avignon (tel: 42 23 45 32), a splendid Provençal farmhouse set in peaceful gardens, with a pool, just northwest of Aix.
Relais Ste-Victoire, Beaurecueil (tel: 42 28 94 98), is a modern building with a pool, set in unspoilt countryside at the southwestern foot of the Montagne Ste-Victoire – a renowned restaurant – it has moderate to expensive rooms. Similar in price is the **Auberge du Belvédère**, Eguilles (tel: 42 92 52 92), a traditional house set in pine woods northwest of Aix. Good-value rooms can be found at **Le Prieuré**, Route de Sisteron (tel: 42 21 05 23), a very peaceful hotel which looks out on the clipped box hedges, plane trees and ornamental pond of the Lenfant park on the northern outskirts of Aix.

Eating Out
Despite its sophistication, Aix has plenty of simple places where you can eat well at reasonable prices. There are lots of café-restaurants in the

streets and squares of Vieil Aix and a great choice of foreign cuisines on offer – everything from Greek to Thai or Peruvian. Dance and music students trying to make ends meet in an expensive city often perform in the street to entertain al fresco diners.

Le Clos de la Violette, 10 Avenue de la Violette, just north of the old centre, serves superbly inventive cuisine, with a regional flavour, which has given it a reputation second to none in Aix – expensive (closed Sunday and Monday lunch). **Les Frères Lani**, 22 Rue Victor Leydet, in Vieil Aix, has a lively choice of dishes and a moderately priced menu (closed Sunday and Monday). Nearby, **La Vieille Auberge**, 63 Rue Espariat, offers a rather cheaper menu of delicious *nouvelle cuisine* (closed Wednesday). **Les Deux Garçons**, 53 Cours Mirabeau, the most stylish café in Aix (and Provence), has long been known as the hang-out for the artistic and intellectual set; inside are gilded mirrors, marble-top tables and old lace curtains while outside there are comfy wicker armchairs in which to sit watching all of Aix stroll by – drinks are expensive on the terrace, but it serves brasserie fare at moderate prices (open until 2am).

At the **Relais Ste Victoire** (see hotels above) you can sample imaginative Provençal cuisine while feasting your eyes on the scenery – menus start at moderate prices. Nearby, at similar rates, **Mas de la Bertrande**, Beaurecueil, is a lovely farmhouse with a pretty terrace serving creative dishes. **Puyfond**, Route St-Canadet, Rigoulon, in peaceful countryside north of Aix (just east of Puyricard), offers tasty fresh cuisine and lower-priced menus (all three closed Sunday dinner and Monday).

Shopping

Vieil Aix is an excellent area for shopping if you have plenty of money. Chic fashion boutiques, with a wealth of designer labels, abound in Rue Espariat, Rue Bédarrides and Rue Aude – including shops for men and children, as well as those selling women's clothes and shoes (at sky-high prices). Also in Rue Espariat is **Comtesse du Barry**, selling regional produce from Provence and Gascony in smart packaging. **Comptoir Anglais du Thé**, Rue Aude, is a tea boutique with fancy tins and teapots. In Rue Méjanes, **Jacquèmes** has a range of herbs, honey, olive oil, wine and Aix's special almond-paste sweets, called *calissons*. **Souleiado** in Place des Tanneurs, and **Les Olivades** in Rue des Chaudronniers both sell traditional Provençal fabrics. **Puyricard**, Rue Rifle-Rafle, has a mouthwatering array of chocolates – among the best in France – made at a traditional factory just north of Aix (on the outskirts of Puyricard village). Towards the north of Vieil Aix, Rue Gaston-de-Saporta has some smart shops, such as **Sesame**, with stylish *objets* for the home including pottery, baskets,

EAST AND CENTRAL BOUCHES-DU-RHONE

wooden ornaments and hammocks, **Aix Antiquities** selling antiques, and **Cremerie Canavese** with more consumable Provençal specialities. Apart from famous designers, familiar names here include **Benetton** and **Bally** – and **Laura Ashley**, in Rue J Cabassol in the Quartier Mazarin. There is also a **Monoprix** store on Cours Mirabeau.

Lots of local artisans make *santon* (Christmas crib) figures and the tourist office (Place du Général-de-Gaulle) has a list of workshops in the area.

Aix is said to have the best **markets** in Provence. A colourful fruit and vegetable market takes place daily in Place Richelme. A magnificent array of every type of local produce can also be found here and in Place des Prêcheurs on Tuesday, Thursday and Saturday. On the same three days there is a flower market on Place Hôtel de Ville, while Place Verdon and the streets around the Palais du Justice have a flea market, clothes and craft stalls.

Place du Général-de-Gaulle

Flowers are also sold on Cours Mirabeau, on Monday, Wednesday and Friday, and in Place Madeleine on Sunday.

Nightlife

Of the clubs in the centre, **Le Richelme**, 24 Rue de la Verrerie, attracts a young crowd, **Le Mistral**, 3 Rue F-Mistral, is popular and upmarket, **Scat**, Rue de la Verrerie, is a jazz club and **Cousin-Germain**, 15 Rue d'Italie, is a café with jazz and blues. In the suburbs, **Hot Brass**, Route d'Eguilles, is the best jazz club in Aix and **La Chimère**, Montée d'Avignon, is a lively gay disco.

Club 88, La Petite Calade, **Oxydium**, Route des Milles, and **Les Templiers**, Lignane, are all discos. **Retro 25**, Pont de Luynes, has different nights for young and older folk while **Années 30**, La Petite Calade, and **Damier**, Avenue des Infirmeries, are clubs for the mature crowd. For details on these and other places (including the casino), ask at the tourist office in Place du Général-de-Gaulle.

Special Events

The best of Aix's many events is the **Festival d'Art Lyrique et de Musique** held in July; details from the Festival Office, Ancien Palais de l'Archevêché (tel: 42 17 34 34). There is also a music festival in June, dance in July, jazz in August, and a Provençal week in July; information from the Comité Officiel des Fêtes, Complexe Forbin, Cours Gambetta (tel: 42 23 37 81).

CASSIS

The most picturesque of the Bouches-du-Rhône's coastal resorts is lively – and very touristy in summer. The old fishing port – frequented by artists earlier this century – nestles below high white cliffs, with villas climbing up the steep slopes around it. Pretty pink and white buildings, with lots of jolly open-air fish restaurants and cafés, line the *quais* beside the engaging harbour full of fishing boats and sleek yachts. In an 18th-century house near the market square is a small local **musée** (*open*: Wednesday to Saturday afternoons). Just south-west are three dramatic *calanques:* long, narrow, fjord-like inlets, where sheer limestone cliffs soar skyward from the translucent turquoise sea. The most spectacular is **En Vau**, which has a shingle beach at the end – reached by boat or footpath along the pine-wooded cliffs. Other *calanques* lie further west, and near the beach resort of La Ciotat to the east. La Ciotat is reached along the Corniche des Crêtes coastal road which climbs steeply and winds along precipitous cliffs – the highest in France (plunging 1,310 feet/399m at Grande Tête) – with superb views from Cap Canaille.

Accommodation

Les Roches Blanches, Route des Calanques (tel: 42 01 09 30), is a creeper-clad house on

Fishing boats and sleek yachts in the harbour at Cassis

a promontory, with fine views, tasteful decor, flowery terraces, a pool and private beach area – moderate to expensive. Also quite expensive is **Le Relais de la Magdeleine**, Gémenos (tel: 42 82 20 05), a beautiful 18th-century Provençal country manor, with a pool, on the outskirts of an attractive little town at the western foot of the Ste-Baume massif.

Eating Out

La Presqu'ile, Port-Miou, is a refined restaurant with a terrace above the sea, at the *calanque* nearest Cassis; it serves light, classic dishes, with menus starting at moderate prices (closed Sunday dinner and Monday, except in July and August).

MARSEILLE

This teeming, traffic-clogged city is not everyone's idea of idyllic Provence, nor a relaxing holiday destination. Even so, its history, as France's first civilised settlement founded by the ancient Greeks, its importance as a major Mediterranean port, and its sheer size, as France's second largest city, make it impossible to ignore. The ugly, industrialised sprawl around the city belies some treasures at its heart.

A visit is likely to start at the **Vieux Port**, a colourful hub of activity, guarded at its entrance by two forts – the medieval **St-Jean** and the 17th-century **St-Nicolas**. The best view of the port is from the **Parc du Pharo** on the south side. The harbour is filled with a forest of bobbing

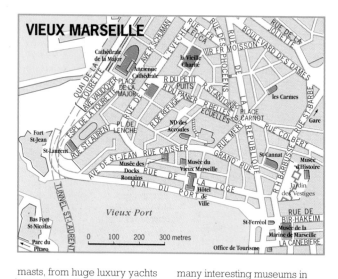

masts, from huge luxury yachts to workaday fishing boats. Pleasure trips run from here along the coast and to the Frioul Islands including **Château d'If**, a forbidding 16th-century castle which was once a prison and from which the fictional Count of Monte Cristo made his legendary escape. Along the lively *quais* are many terraced restaurants where you can sample the famous Provençal fish stew, *bouillabaisse*.

The narrow, crumbling, dirty streets of **Le Panier** climb a hill north of the port; this is the site of the original Greek city of *Massalia*. Perched on a bluff to the south is the impressive landmark of **Notre-Dame-de-la-Garde**, a 19th-century neo-Byzantine basilica.

Running east from the Vieux Port is the central thoroughfare, **La Canebière**, with the main tourist office at No 4. There are many interesting museums in the city. The **Musée des Docks Romains**, by the Vieux Port, is built over the excavated remains of the Roman docks. The **Musée du Vieux Marseille**, in Rue de la Prison, explains popular local arts and traditions. The **Musée Grobet-Labadie**, Boulevard Longchamp, houses fine antique furniture, tapestries, musical instruments and ceramics.

The historic monuments of Marseille include the fortified **Basilique St-Victor**, by the port, dating from the 5th and 11th centuries, and the **Jardin des Vestiges**, a garden containing excavated Greek remains.

Eating Out

Les Arcenaulx, 25 Cours d'Estienne-d'Orves, on a spacious square just south of the Vieux Port, serves simple but creative dishes at moderate rates (closed Sunday and Monday dinner). **Chez Madie**, 138 Quai du Port, has a terrace overlooking the harbour and offers delicious Provençal fish specialities at reasonable prices (closed Sunday dinner and Monday). Two highly recommended, pricier restaurants are the **Miramar**, 12 Quai du Port, and **Passedat**, Corniche Kennedy, Anse de Maldormé (at the Petit Nice hotel by the sea to the south).

◆◆
SALON-DE-PROVENCE
This low-key town sits at the heart of Bouches-du-Rhône, on the eastern edge of the arid Crau plain – where a canal was constructed in the 16th century by the local engineer, Adam de Craponne, to irrigate the area. Another celebrated 16th-century inhabitant was the astrologer, Nostradamus. Salon is now an important market town for olive oil.

The Old Port, Marseille

The main gateway into the **Vieille Ville** lies opposite the plane-shaded Place Crousillat, where pleasant pavement cafés are set by a moss and fern-covered fountain. The **Port de l'Horloge** is an ornate 17th-century clock-tower and passing through its archway you meet a huge mural of Nostradamus. The old town is dominated by the crenellated towers of the imposing medieval fortress, the **Château de l'Empiri**, which was once the residence of the archbishops of Arles. It now houses a **museum** of French military history, from the time of Louis XVI to 1918 (*closed:* Tuesday).
The simple, stone **Eglise St-Michel** has 12th-century carvings over the door. Nearby is the excellent Maison Nostradamus, in the astrologer's former home, which explains much about his life and times (*open:* afternoons except Tuesday). His tomb can be seen in the 14th and 15th-century

gothic **Collegiale St-Laurent**, just north of the Vieille Ville.
On the eastern edge of town, on Avenue de Pisavi, is the **Musée de Salon et de la Crau**, a large 19th-century house with varied displays of natural history, local art, furniture, costumes and soap-making, a traditional industry using olive oil (*closed:* Saturday and Sunday morning, and Tuesday).

Nearby
Hidden among the rocks and pines of the Montagne du Defens, north of Salon, are the **Grottes de Calès**, a troglodyte village inhabited from neolithic times up to the Middle Ages. You can explore the natural and man-made caves. Nearby, the traditional small town of **Eyguières** has many ancient buildings.
East of Salon, the **Château de la Barben** is a magnificent 17th-century castle built on a bluff, with sumptuous furnishings inside and a zoo in the grounds. (Castle *closed:* Tuesday from September to May).

The ingredients of a traditional Provençal bouillabaisse

Accommodation
The **Abbaye de Ste-Croix**, Val de Cuech (tel: 90 56 24 55), dates back to the 9th century and is set in the rocky, pine-wooded hills just northeast of Salon. The decor is simple and traditional, in keeping with the tranquillity of the buildings. There are stunning views from the dining terrace and a pool in the gardens – expensive.

SILVACANE, ABBAYE DE
Lying on a verdant slope overlooking the river Durance, this is one of the great 12th-century Cistercian abbeys of Provence. The compact, weathered buildings have a sober beauty – the only adornment to be seen is in the vast refectory, rebuilt in the 15th century.
Open: April to September, 09.00–19.00hrs; October to March, 09.00–12.00 and 14.00–17.00hrs. *Closed:* Tuesday, October to March.

VAR AND ALPES-DE-HAUTE-PROVENCE

This eastern part of Provence does not have the wealth of major historic monuments to be found to the west, but it does have splendid scenery and picturesque old villages; it is also a fine area for walking, climbing, horse-riding and watersports (on the coast or on the many man-made lakes inland). Inland you will find the typical Provençal palette of rustic tones with shades of timeless tranquillity. In small towns and villages the inhabitants continue with age-old occupations, producing wine, honey, herbs, lavender, olive oil, goat's cheese or pottery. The frenetic pace of urban life seems worlds away.

Rooftops and rocky cliffs at Cotignac

CENTRAL VAR VILLAGES

The busy A8 autoroute cuts right across the centre of the Var connecting Aix to the Côte d'Azur but it is only a short drive north from this road to a group of unspoilt villages. Just 12 miles (20km) north of the A8 is **Cotignac**, a charming, shady village with tall painted stucco or bare stone houses snuggled together on the valley slopes below rocky cliffs and the remaining towers of an ancient castle. From the picturesque Place de la Mairie, a little street leads up to the clocktower, church and gardens, with a path to caves in the cliff which contain interesting water-sculpted rock formations. Heading east, you pass through extensive vineyards en route to **Entrecasteaux**. At the centre of this enticing village, is a

beautiful 17th-century château. This was recently renovated by the Scottish avant-garde artist, Ian McGarvie-Munn and is very simply decorated with his paintings (*open:* daily). Northwest of Cotignac is the delectable *vieux village* of **Fox-Amphoux** crowning a steep, wooded hill; here the 16th-century priory has been converted into a small hotel, the Auberge du Vieux Fox (see below). It is very tranquil with ethereal views of distant mountains.

Tourtour (about 12 miles/20km east of Fox-Amphoux) is an enchanting village of ancient rough-stone houses, adorned with age-old creeper, set around a tree-lined square with a fountain and a couple of lively cafés. Its allure, combined with breathtaking views, ensures that many summer visitors find their way here, but its character remains unspoilt.

Nestling beneath a rocky cliff in the valley below is the lovely village of **Villecroze**. Its delightful old quarter, reached through a clock-tower archway, is enlivened by colourful pot plants, little fountains and cats prowling along the narrow alleys. Beside the cliff are green, leafy gardens with a waterfall and water-formed caves which can be visited. Other appealing old villages in the area include **Aups**, **Barjols** and **Châteaudouble**. Also in the region is the superb 12th-century Cistercian **Abbaye du Thoronet** (*closed:* Tuesday), with its cloister, church and chapterhouse surrounded by woods and vineyards.

Accommodation

La Bastide, Tourtour (tel: 94 70 57 30), is a fine stone mansion set on wooded slopes just outside the village, with superb views and a pool– expensive. **Lou Calen**, Cotignac (tel: 94 04 60 40), set on the main square, is full of traditional charm and atmosphere and it has a pool; room prices are reasonable to expensive. The **Auberge du Vieux Fox**, Fox-Amphoux (tel: 94 80 71 69), is a simple tranquil *Logis* in a 16th-century priory with wonderful views and rooms at very reasonable rates plus good-value menus. **Des Deux Rocs**, Place Font d'Amont, Seillans (tel: 94 76 87 32), is a tasteful 18th-century house in the old quarter with prices ranging from very reasonable to quite expensive.

◆◆◆
GRAND CANYON DU VERDON

The Verdon river forms the boundary between the Var to the south and the Alpes-de-Haute-Provence to the north. Where the river cuts through the mountainous Plâteau de Valensole it has formed a canyon so magnificent that it makes the other grand gorges of Provence look like a mere scratch on the landscape. Towering crags and soaring cliffs of crumpled limestone thrust up to 4,920 feet (1,500m) each side of the gorge. The well-named **Corniche Sublime** road snakes along the southern rock faces, while the **Route des**

The dramatic limestone cliffs of the Grand Canyon du Verdon

Crêtes clings to the northern ridge. Both offer heart-stopping, hair-raising panoramas, with sheer drops plunging over 1,640 feet (500m) down to the thin trickle of the river below. The precipitous hair-pin bends, narrow roads and vertiginous views demand careful driving, and either route will take at least half a day.

The most dramatic way to see the gorge is to walk along the bottom, where the gap between the cliffs is no more than 20 feet (6m) wide in places – and where the river is, in turn, a languid deep blue or a tumble of white water. Information on guided tours lasting from two hours and up to three days can be obtained at the tourist offices in Moustiers-Ste-Marie or La Palud-sur-Verdon, along with advice on canoeing, climbing, bicycling, horse-riding and other activities. Watersports are also popular on the man-made **Lac de Ste-Croix**, a huge expanse of glistening turquoise water at the western end of the Canyon.

Moustiers-Ste-Marie, spectacularly set on a sheer rocky hillside just north of the lake, has become a busy base for visits to the Canyon, but for centuries it has been famed for its glazed pottery. Pottery workshops and souvenir shops line the steep, narrow streets and some of the best examples of this local craft can be seen in the Musée de la Faïence (*closed:* Tuesday), opposite the Romanesque church with its graceful belfry.

Lying in a high valley further to the west is the charming little town of **Riez**, where lavender and honey are important products. The old quarter has some rich Renaissance façades within the remains of the medieval ramparts. There is also a small museum, a 5th-century baptistry and the remains of a Roman temple. About 5 miles (8km) southwest is the village of **Allemagne-en-Provence**, with its beautiful château dating from the 14th to the 16th century (*open:* Friday to Sunday, from 16.00hrs).

Accommodation

At the east end of the Grand Canyon, the **Château de Trigance** (tel: 94 76 91 18) is an 11th-century fortress set on a rocky hill above the village of Trigance with marvellous views of the austere countryside. The hotel is full of medieval splendour and atmosphere but is quite expensive.

◆◆
SOUTHWEST ALPES-DE-HAUTE-PROVENCE

This area can easily be visited as an excursion from Vaucluse, and the scenery shares certain characteristics with that of the eastern Lubéron and Plâteau de Vaucluse, across the border. The tranquil town of **Forcalquier** is clustered on a wooded hill crowned by the remains of its medieval citadel, with a crumbling old quarter south of the cathedral. To the south is the medieval hill village of **Mane**. Just outside lies a Benedictine priory, **Notre-Dame-de-Salagon**, a 12th-century fortified Romanesque church, surrounded by later buildings, which now houses

VAR & ALPES-DE-HAUTE-PROVENCE

the **Conservatoire Ethnologique** – an interesting museum and garden showing how the region's traditional ways of life have developed (*open:* afternoons only April to early November). Further south is the **Château de Sauvan**, an elegantly aristocratic 18th-century mansion with grand furnishings, which is a surprising gem of refinement in this rough and ready terrain (*open:* from 15.30 hrs, *closed:* Saturday). Just to the west are the gleaming white domes of the **Observatoire-de-Haute-Provence**, a scientific research station for astronomers in a site chosen for the clarity of the air and the sky.

Haute-Provence has its quota of picturesque perched villages – many seem quite untouched by the 20th century. Located in the wooded countryside around Forcalquier, **Lurs** is a lovely village clustered on a high ledge below its castle, overlooking the Durance valley. **Dauphin** is another delightful fortified *village perché*. To the

northwest is the superbly atmospheric **Simiane-la-Rotonde**, surrounded by mountain slopes and lavender fields below the domed remains of its castle. Towards the Montagne de Lure, is the ancient huddle of **Banon**, famed for its goat's cheese. **Reillanne** is another appealing, sleepy hill village further south, near the Parc Naturel Régional du Lubéron.

Accommodation
The **Auberge de Reillanne** (tel: 92 76 45 95), is a lovely, peaceful 18th-century farmhouse set in a shady garden just outside the village of Reillanne, with views of the Lubéron, offering rustic rooms at quite reasonable rates.

The clear air and tumbling terrain of Forcalquier

Peace and Quiet

Wildlife and Countryside in Provence by Paul Sterry

Provence is a land of stunning beauty, boasting a marvellous variety of wildlife, from sheets of spring flowers to hosts of waterbirds. In addition to the array of wild flowers, there are fields of attractive herbs grown for their scent and flavour. Indeed, the smell of Provence lingers as long in the mind as does its appearance.

The Camargue, a vast area of wetland sited in the Rhône delta, is probably the best-known wildlife location in Provence, but there are other, equally exciting, landscapes, including rolling limestone hills, in places cloaked in woodland, and classic, colourful Mediterranean flora. Over the millennia, rivers such as the Ardèche and the Verdon have left their mark in the form of dramatic gorges carved into the bedrock.

The wealth of flowers, both wild and cultivated, is reflected in the insect life: butterflies are seemingly everywhere, in all shapes, sizes and colours, while beetles, bugs, bees and moths complete the array. In short, Provence is a naturalist's paradise.

The Camargue

The Camargue is one of the premier birdwatching locations in Europe and most ornithologists make a pilgrimage to this world-famous wetland at some time. The region comprises the delta of the Rhône, and the Camargue Regional Park is more-or-less defined by the triangle formed by the two arms of the river as they head towards the Mediterranean south of Arles. This vast area is a classic river delta, formed where the Rhône meets the Mediterranean. A network of shallow lagoons (called *étangs*) bounded by marshland, have built up and, generally speaking, the closer they lie to the sea, the more saline they are. This gradation of aquatic conditions, from saline lagoons to freshwater marsh and reedbed, is one of the secrets of the Camargue's richness and diversity. The presence of a whole spectrum of aquatic environments means that almost all European wetland birds, not to mention mammals, amphibians and insects, can find somewhere suitable within its boundaries.

PEACE AND QUIET

Flamingos

Greater flamingos are perhaps *the* most characteristic birds of the Camargue and it is these which most visitors hope to see. No-one could mistake these huge, pink extraordinary birds. Everything about them is precisely adapted to the habitat that many of the region's *étangs* provide – saline water, rich in small invertebrate life; those odd-looking bills are used upside down to filter food from the water while the long legs enable them to wade into deeper water than other species. Although flamingos are invariably present in the Camargue, their numbers are variable and unpredictable. Because of their precise feeding requirements, any change in food availability may mean that the birds suddenly move on to new territories. And it is that food which gives them their pink tinge; without it they become merely white.

At the area's heart is the **Etang de Vaccarès** national reserve, which cannot be entered without a permit. However, this central reserve can easily be overlooked from surrounding roads and there are plenty of alternative *étangs* and areas of dried saltmarsh worthy of scrutiny.

Visitors to the Camargue usually stay either in Arles, 12 miles (20km) from the Etang de Vaccarès, or in Les Saintes-Maries-de-la-Mer, on the coast.

The D570 runs between the two towns and there is a park information centre 3 miles (5km) north of the coast at **Ginès**. There is another centre on the east side of the reserve on the D36b at **La Capelière**, together with a nature trail. The best way to explore the Camargue is to drive the roads surrounding the Etang de Vaccarès and stop at suitable vantage points. Particularly good areas on the west side are on the road north of **Stes-Maries**, where smaller *étangs*

lie beside the road, and at **Cacharel**, 4 miles (6km) further north. The northern shores of the Etang de Vaccarès can be seen from **Méjanes** and near **Mas d'Agon** on the D37 roughly 12 miles (20km) south of Arles. On the eastern side, **La Capelière** offers good opportunities for observation, and the saltpans to the south of **Salin-de-Giraud** can be particularly good for flamingos.

The Camargue has something to offer birdwatchers at any time of year. In winter, tens of thousands of ducks arrive from northern Europe, while in summer, herons, egrets, waders and flamingos breed here. Larks and stone curlews also nest here, favouring dry saltmarsh dominated by glasswort and sea lavender. Additionally, during the spring and autumn migrations, vast numbers of other birds stop off to feed and rest before resuming their travels.

Saltwater inlets and marshland of the Camargue

PEACE AND QUIET

Cultivated sage

Mediterranean Flowers

In spring, the Mediterranean region in general, and Provence in particular, bursts into green life and a vast array of flowers greets the eye. Much of the vegetation is adapted to the climate of the region – dry, hot summers and cool, damp winters – and so most of the flowering is concentrated into the months of April and May. One of the special delights of Provence is the *maquis* habitat, where shrubs and scattered trees harbour a wealth of plant life. Known equally for their fragrance, there are junipers, rosemary, thyme and sage, as well as tree heathers, brooms, cistuses and spurges. In some areas, orchids are abundant. Provence orchid, lady orchid and sword-leaved helleborine are among the larger species, while members of the bee orchid family are also well represented.

La Grande Crau

La Grande Crau is a region of arid, semi-desert east of the Camargue. The stony landscape is brought to life in spring by colourful flowers characteristic of *garrigue*-type habitats, including thymes, cistuses, spurges and asphodels. Although much reduced in area due to changes in land use, La Grande Crau is still good for dry-country birds such as little bustards, pin-tailed sandgrouse, black-eared wheatears and several species of larks.

The best way to explore La Grande Crau is to take the D568 which runs southeast from Arles to Fos-sur-Mer. Some 19 miles (30km) from Arles, the habitat starts to become good – take minor roads and tracks northeast from the road and stop at suitable points to explore the habitat. Early mornings are best, especially when searching for birds such as the sandgrouse. Flocks can be seen flying to and from watering places on the plain.

Les Alpilles

This chain of limestone hills lies north of the Camargue and Arles, with St-Rémy-de-Provence at its northern edge. The area is best explored by taking roads south from St-Rémy: the D5 heads towards Maussane-les-Alpilles with a side road leading to the viewpoint at **La Caume**, while the D27 goes close to **Les Baux-de-Provence**, about 5 miles (8km) south of St Rémy and a good, if popular, spot to start exploring the region. Swifts are a familiar sight in the skies above Les Alpilles and in villages like Les Baux. In addition to common swifts, look for the paler pallid swifts and the larger alpine swifts which have white throats and bellies. Birds of prey are among the highlights of a visit to this area, while the rich *maquis* vegetation harbours several species of warblers as well as hoopoes and blue rock thrushes in more open areas.

Parc Naturel Régional du Lubéron

The Lubéron Regional Park lies in the east of the region and is a range of limestone hills with quintessential Provençal views and landscapes. More than 463 square miles (1,200 sq km) in extent, the park is bordered to the east by Manosque and to the west by Cavaillon. It was established to protect and preserve both the landscape

Bee-eaters

These are undoubtedly the most colourful birds in the region. Their plumage is a mixture of orange, yellow, green, blue and black, and their graceful, gliding flight is just as elegant as their appearance. They are summer visitors to Europe, arriving in April and May and flying south to Africa in September. They nest in burrows excavated in sandy banks and small colonies of these beautiful birds can sometimes be seen in roadside banks or cuttings. As their name suggests, they feed on insects – especially bees, flies and dragonflies – which are caught on the wing.

and the local communities. The park is bisected by the Combe de Lourmarin which runs from Apt in the north (where there is a park information centre) to Lourmarin in the south: the area east of the Combe is called the Grand Lubéron while that to the west is the Petit Lubéron. To explore the Grand Lubéron take the road from Apt to Lourmarin and stop at suitable vantage points to explore the terrain. The village of **Buoux**, 4 miles (7km) south of Apt, and **Buoux Fort** are good starting points. Also, the views from **Mourre Nègre** are superb. Take the D48 east from Apt towards Castellet and Céreste. Park in Auribeau, 6 miles (10km) southeast of Apt. Retrace your steps and take the track to Mourre Nègre. The Petit Lubéron is best explored

PEACE AND QUIET

by taking the D3 west from Apt through Bonnieux and Ménerbes towards Cavaillon. The northern and southern slopes of the Lubéron range show contrasting vegetation types; the southern slopes have essentially Mediterranean habitats of *garrigue* and *maquis*, while on the north there are more extensive woodlands of oak, cedar and beech among others.

Salvia grown for perfume

Wild flowers are abundant in spring and early summer with the southern limestone slopes in particular favouring brooms, lavenders, cistuses and a wide range of orchid species. Warblers and other insect-eating birds thrive in this habitat and lizards and snakes also do well, feeding on the abundant invertebrate life. Birdwatchers should scan the skies at frequent intervals for birds of prey, including short-toed eagles and booted eagles.

Birds of Prey

The hills and gorges that characterise so much of Provence provide ideal habitats for birds of prey. Sunny slopes provide warm updraughts on which they can soar, and more retiring species find ideal, secluded nest sites in the steep, rocky gorges. Among the more interesting species is the peregrine, an elegant falcon that is renowned for its speed in flight. Gorges and ravines are their preferred habitats. Short-toed eagles, on the other hand, prefer sunny slopes with open country or woodland clearings where their prey – snakes and lizards – bask in the open. You may even be lucky enough to see one in flight with a snake trailing from its beak as it returns to the nest to feed its young.

Grand Canyon du Verdon

Situated in eastern Provence, this gorge is one of the most dramatic natural sights in the region. Over the millenia, the River Verdon has carved a winding cleft through the limestone bedrock; in places it is over 144 feet (44m) deep. To reach it, drive north east from Aix-en-Provence for about 19 miles (30km) and then take the D952 to **Moustiers-Ste-Marie** at the western end of the gorge. Beyond the village the road forks, one route passing along the northern side of the gorge, the other along the southern. Avoid peak tourist periods because of numbers of visitors.

Birdwatchers should stop and scan the gorge in places for crag martins. These unassuming brown birds are only found in rocky habitats such as the Verdon gorge and small groups are often seen hawking for insects on the wing, close to the cliff face. Alpine swifts also occur here and are much more impressive fliers. Their streamlined appearance and conspicuous black plumage, with contrasting white throat and belly, make them easy to identify as they hunt for insects. Less aerobatic, but no less attractive, is the blue rock thrush, males of which are indeed deep blue. They are most easily located by listening for the rather mournful song, sung from exposed rocky outcrops and ledges on the slopes.

Ardèche Valley

A drive along the course of the Ardèche Valley offers several opportunities to see spectacular limestone scenery – in particular a majestic gorge – carved over the centuries by the course of the river. There are extensive and superb woods on the way which make an interesting diversion from the views of the gorge. The route can be crowded at peak holiday times.

From Vallon-Pont-d'Arc, in the northwest, take the D290 which runs along the course of the gorge. After 3 miles (5km) stop at **Pont d'Arc** and walk down to the arch through which the river flows. Look for birds such as dippers and grey wagtails close to the water and alpine

PEACE AND QUIET

Greater flamingos and their offspring

swifts and peregrines in the skies above. Continue along the road, stopping at the numerous viewpoints *(belvédères)* that have been provided. Scan the skies for birds of prey and explore the oak woodlands for orchids and birds, including blackcaps and golden orioles. As dusk approaches you may hear the strange call of the Scop's owl, which sounds just like the 'blip' of a sonar instrument.

Mont Ventoux

Mont Ventoux lies in northern Provence close to the D938 between Nyons and Carpentras. The mountain rises to nearly 6,562 feet (2,000 m) and offers superb views across the Rhône valley. The D974 ascends the mountain from **Malaucène** where it leaves the D938. Stop at intervals en route to admire the view and to scan the skies for birds of prey. It is roughly 12 miles (20km) from Malaucene to the summit of Mont Ventoux but, obviously,

the steepness of the terrain means that you will not want, or be able , to drive quickly.

Herbes de Provence
Provençal cooking is famous for its use of an array of herbs. While some of these are grown commercially, most have their origins in the native flora, and many are still harvested from the wild. Classic species include rosemary, thyme, marjoram, basil and taragon, typical members of the aromatic habitat known as *maquis*. This shrubby mixture of low-growing herbs, shrubs and pockets of small trees is typical of sunny hillsides and the aroma associated with it is memorable. *Maquis* is a habitat that has been strongly influenced by man – centuries of tree clearance for timber and firewood have encouraged the *maquis* flowers and shrubs, many of which, had the forest not been cleared, would have been typical of woodland clearings.

Practical

This section (with the yellow band) includes food,drink, shopping, accommodation, nightlife,tight budget, special events etc.

FOOD AND DRINK

The food and wines of Provence provide an endless source of pleasure. For some, they are the major reason for visiting the area.

Restaurants

You can eat well in Provençal restaurants without spending a fortune – in fact this is one of the few aspects of Provence where bargains are to be found. Most restaurants provide a choice of fixed-price menus which are displayed outside, ranging from a basic three-course meal to more elaborate and more expensive gourmet feasts. Some also offer a special low-priced lunch menu. As a rule, it is cheaper to go for a set-price menu than to choose dishes from the *à la carte* menu. Provence also has some great gourmet establishments which attract people from far and wide; they include **L'Oustau de Baumanière** at Les Baux, **Hiély-Lucullus** in Avignon and **Passédat** in Marseille. In such places, the prices may be high but the menus may still be good value when the quality of the ingredients and the standard of

the cuisine is taken into account. Many of the hotels listed in this guide also have good restaurants that are well worth trying.

One of the best ways to savour a Provençal meal is to sit outside, and many restaurants have a sunny terrace shaded by parasols, plane trees or vine-covered pergolas. The best places are always popular, so do not leave it too late to find a table. People tend to eat early: lunch is served from about 12.00hrs and dinner from 19.00 or 19.30hrs. Sunday lunch is the big meal of the week. Even if you enjoy self-catering, using the wealth of fresh produce available, it is still well worth splashing out on a restaurant meal now and again to try some real Provençal specialities.

Food

Dishes described as *à la provençale* generally include olive oil, garlic, tomatoes and herbs, such as rosemary, thyme and basil. The local *ail*, (garlic) is a gentle variety; the blazing red tomatoes (or *pommes d'amour*, 'love apples') are

FOOD AND DRINK

bursting with flavour. These typically rich, fragrant, sun-kissed ingredients are designed to enhance rather than disguise the taste of the food. The most celebrated Provençal dish is *bouillabaisse*, a soupy stew made from different fish and shellfish, cooked in an aromatic *bouillon* (stock) which includes herbs, saffron, fennel and garlic. It is served with toast and *rouille*, a red spicy mayonnaise (made with red peppers, saffron and garlic). *Bouillabaisse* at its best can be found around the Vieux Port in Marseille – but it is not cheap, here or anywhere else. *Bourride* is another classic dish, a white- fish soup or stew traditionally served with *aïoli*, a garlic and olive oil mayonnaise – which also transforms *hors-d'oeuvre* and vegetables (especially raw *crudités*). *Estocaficada* is stockfish stew with tomatoes, olives, peppers, garlic and onions. *Brandade* is salt cod pounded into a creamy paste with olive oil, milk and garlic. *Tapenade*, a superb purée of black olives, anchovies and capers, and *anchoïade*, anchovy paste, are often used as sauces (for fish, meat or pasta).

Coastal restaurants offer a glorious range of fish: one of the tastiest is *rouget* (red mullet) and a white fish, such as *loup de mer* (sea bass) is delicious cooked in fennel. The array of *fruits de mer* and *crustacés* is equally enticing – from *langoustes* (spiny lobsters) to *oursins* (sea urchins) and *tellines* (tiny clams from the Camargue). Inland you are more likely to be offered freshwater fish, such as

truite (trout) or *catigau*, a dish of *anguilles* (eels) in a garlic and red wine sauce.

Lamb often features on the menu – including the herby, spicy *agneau de Sisteron*, from the mountain pastures, and the delicate *agneau de pré-salé*, lamb grazed on salt-marshes. Beef is less common, but around the Camargue *boeuf à la gardianne* is popular – a rich stew, similar to *boeuf en daube*, cooked with red wine, herbs, garlic, vegetables and black olives. *Pieds et paquets* (trotters and tripe) is a speciality of Marseille, and Arles has its *saucissons* (sausages).

Salads and vegetables are usually served as a separate course. *Salade niçoise* is a meal in itself, composed of green salad, tomatoes, onions, peppers, beans, black olives, anchovies and sometimes tuna and egg. *Mesclun* is a salad combining several different leaves. *Ratatouille* is a luscious vegetable stew, including aubergines, onions, tomatoes and courgettes cooked in olive oil, herbs and garlic. Stuffed vegetables, such as *tomates farcies*, are common. In late autumn and winter all sorts of wonderful mushrooms and fungi – including the much-prized truffles – come from the woods. The Italian influence is strong, and pasta dishes abound; a classic sauce is *pistou*, made with basil, garlic and olive oil – it is also used to flavour vegetable soup. Pizza is very popular, and tomatoes, black olives and anchovies are among the typical toppings. There are also local dishes using rice from the

Camargue; *riz* (or *salade camarguais*) is a risotto made with *calmar* (squid), *crevettes* (prawns) and *moules* (mussels). Cheese is served before the dessert, and the best local varieties are made from goat's or ewe's milk – such as *Banon*, wrapped in vine or chestnut leaves, and the herby, peppery *poivre d'âne*. The selection of melt-in-the-mouth pastries, fruit flans and tarts are much too delectable to turn down. The fields and orchards of Provence produce a lavish variety of fruit, including figs, cherries, grapes, pears, peaches, strawberries

Melting egg-rich pastry used to make a flan base

and the small, sweet melons with which the market town of Cavaillon is synonymous. *Pastèque à la Provençal* is chilled watermelon filled with red or rosé wine – most refreshing.
Various simple snacks are available in cafés, or to take away from a wealth of *pâtisseries*, full of tempting treats. Apart from the sweet pastries, savoury snacks include *pan bagnat* (bread with olive oil, anchovies, tomatoes and peppers), *pissaladière* (a pizza-like flan), *fougasse* (bread containing olives, anchovies, sausage or cheese and fragrant flavouring) and vegetable tarts. *Charcuteries* also have a

delicious range of ready-made dishes and salads. Picnickers and self-caterers can assemble sumptuous feasts by visiting one of the many markets (and supermarkets), where there are dazzling displays of fruit and vegetables, and a tantalising choice of other delicacies including cheese, ham (such as *jambon cru* or *de campagne*), paté, olives (some of the best come from around Nyons), jars of lavender honey and *tapenade* (a purée of black savoury olives, anchovies and capers). For those with a sweet tooth, there are various specialities: *glacé* (crystallised) fruits (and jam) from Apt, *calissons*, almond-paste *petits fours*, from Aix, *berlingots*, delicate caramels, from Carpentras, melon *confits* from Avignon and nougat from several places, such as Sault.

Drink

Wine has been a traditional part of Provençal life since time immemorial. Most famous are the red Côtes du Rhône wines, especially the classy, full-bodied (and highly priced) Châteauneuf-du-Pape. Gigondas, in the Dentelles, also produces a distinguished wine which is dark and strong. Nearby, Beaumes-de-Venise is renowned for its sweet muscat. From just across the Rhône, in Gard, come the fine rosés of Tavel and Lirac. The Listel *grain-de-gris* rosé is a *vin des sables* from vines grown in sand near Aigues-Mortes.

Rustic simplicity, the keynote of Provençal cuisine

The dry whites from Cassis and the strong red and whites from Bandol (further east along the coast) are also worth trying. Other wines from this region, which include some inexpensive but very drinkable varieties, are Côtes de Provence, Coteaux de Tricastin (from the Valreàs enclave in north Vaucluse), Côtes de Ventoux, Côtes de Lubéron, Coteaux d'Aix and Coteaux du Var.

Vineyards are found all over Provence and there are plenty of opportunities for visiting the *caves* or *domaines* to taste the wine and buy directly from the *vignerons* or from the local Maisons du Vin or Coopératives Vinicoles. For further information contact the Comité Interprofessional des Vins: for Côtes du Rhône, Maison du Tourism et du Vin, 41 Cours Jean-Jaurès, 84000 Avignon (tel: 90 27 24 00); and for Côtes de Provence, Maison des Vins, 83460 Les Arcs-sur-Argens (tel: 94 73 33 38). Otherwise local tourist offices can help.

The aniseed-flavoured *pastis* – such as Ricard, Pastis 51 or Pernod – is a popular Provençal aperitif, drunk with ice and water. Another local aperitif is St-Raphaël, either a sweet red or drier white.

Herb or honey liqueurs can be found especially in mountain areas such as Haut-Var or the Haute-Provence. Some monasteries produce their own concoctions, such as the pungent herb liqueur Sénancole from Sénanque. Among the usual range of soft

FOOD AND DRINK / SHOPPING

drinks, *citron pressé* with fresh lemon juice (or *orange pressé*) is very refreshing. Perrier is a famous local mineral water – the source and factory is between Nîmes and Aigues-Mortes. Coffee is strong and aromatic – unless you want it black, ask for *café au lait* or *café crème*. Otherwise you could try the delicious *chocolat chaud*, hot chocolate, or one of the many herbal teas.

SHOPPING

Provence offers an excellent choice of shopping, from the ultra-high chic of Avignon and Aix to the weekly markets held in many villages and towns. Market day is a great social occasion when the streets come to life in endless colourful tableaux, full of local characters in animated conversation and the sound of street performers – not to mention the smell of herbs and fruit, fresh coffee and sizzling pizzas.

Food and drink specialities which are worth taking home from Provence include wine, olive oil (which you can buy directly from the oil mills – ask at tourist offices for details), *herbes de Provence* (St-Rémy is an important centre for herbs), garlic, honey, jam and, of course, the various local speciality sweets.

Other traditional Provençal products include lavender, *eau de toilette*, dried flowers, pot-pourri, soap, scented candles and herbal cosmetics. Perfume is also popular – the main centre is just outside Provence in Grasse, north of Cannes, where you can visit the factories. The **Musée des Aromes et du Parfum**, northwest of St-Rémy, also sells perfume.

There are numerous local artisans' workshops and artists' galleries to look around. Some of the pottery is irresistible – from decorative pieces made with real panache (Ansouis, Oppède-le-Vieux and Venasque all have interesting little shops) to sturdy, rustic cookware (try the **Poterie Provençal** in Aubagne). Other typical crafts include artefacts of olive wood or cork, basketry, glassware, hand-woven wool garments, and leather (especially from the Camargue).

Santons are figurines that were originally used in Christmas crib scenes in homes when the churches were closed during the period of the French Revolution. They have since become an important Provençal tradition, embracing many popular characters apart from the usual Nativity figures. They are widely sold, and tourist offices can direct you to the workshops of the makers, or *santonniers*.

Traditional Provençal cottons printed with distinctive designs can either be bought by the length or ready-made into a range of colourful clothes and furnishings, from shirts and skirts to cushion covers and quilts. These are sold in various places, but most famous are the two Provençal shops **Souleiado** (meaning 'sunbeam' in Provençal) and **Les Olivades**, which have branches in Avignon, Aix and Arles.

ACCOMMODATION

The sunkissed olive

The hotels recommended in this guide have been chosen for their quality, ambience and value for money, though some are very modern, the majority exude traditional Provençal charm and character. Many are small, personal and set in old buildings. It is essential to book well in advance for the summer months – especially in July and August. At other times of the year, you should be able to find rooms without booking. However, it is always worth telephoning in advance, since many hotels close for a month or more during autumn or winter.

Room prices are partly dictated by the hotel's star rating (from one to four stars, plus L for the most luxurious) but it is worth remembering that even the top-rated hotels sometimes have less expensive rooms and vice versa. In the high season some hotels charge higher prices or insist on *demi-pension* (half-board) terms, which means you are expected to dine at the hotel. When looking at prices, check whether the local tax is included – the amount depends on the hotel grade and the local authority.

Some of the smaller, cheaper hotels, especially in towns, do not have restaurants and just provide breakfast. As breakfast is usually charged separately from the room, you can choose to go to a nearby café instead (which will often be cheaper). All but the cheapest rooms have a private bathroom or a shower and toilet. Many hotels have a pool, and some of the more upmarket ones offer other sports facilities, such as tennis or horse-riding. Some hotels listed in the **What to See** section are described as *Logis*. This means that they belong to the Logis de France association, whose members provide an excellent range of reliable, lower-priced hotels – most have restaurants and serve consistently good food.

Overseas branches of the French Government Tourist

Office (see page 124) can supply details of this and other hotel groups and a full list of hotels in Provence.

It is often worth contacting local or regional tourist offices in Provence, as well, for details on other types of accommodation. Bed and breakfast, (*chambre d'hôte*), can be a reasonably priced and appealing alternative to a hotel, especially in an atmospheric old farmhouse in the countryside. *Gîtes d'étape* provide basic, budget accommodation, often in dormitories, and are found especially in hiking and cycling areas. Mountain refuge huts offer the bare minimum, but can be useful in an emergency; they are usually open only in summer.

Self-catering

The Gîtes de France organisation offers all sorts of self-catering accommodation – from simple rustic dwellings to luxurious villas with all the trimmings. Prices are highest in July and August. Brochures and booking forms are available from the main tourist office in each *département* (see **Tourist Offices** in the **Directory**). The same brochures also list *chambres d'hôte*, *gîtes d'étape*, *fermes auberges*, *camping à la ferme* and other types of accommodation – and they explain how to make advance reservations.

Camping

There are plenty of campsites in Provence, and most have good facilities (see page 113). If you are staying well inland, booking is less imperative than for anywhere near the coast, where campsites soon become packed out in summer – and tend to be more expensive. Local tourist offices have lists so you can phone ahead to ensure there is room if you have not booked. Many close in the low season.

CULTURE, ENTERTAINMENT AND NIGHTLIFE

Provence is not renowned for its throbbing discos and lively nightlife – so you can hang up your dancing shoes, unless you are staying near one of the main towns or coastal resorts, and even here, the nightclubs and discos often operate at weekends only. If you are searching for glitz and glamour after dark, head for the Côte d'Azur instead. In Provence, socialising mostly takes place in cafés – there are some in Aix and Avignon that offer live jazz. On the cultural front, by contrast, Provence really comes into its own (see **Special Events**, page 107). Avignon, Aix and Marseille all have resident theatre companies and orchestras; Avignon and Marseille also have an opera house. Concerts, often in churches, take place throughout the year in the main towns. Many places have cinemas showing undubbed foreign films.

There are casinos in Aix, Cassis and in the coastal resorts further east. Tourist offices have information on nightclubs and often provide free listings pamphlets; otherwise local papers give details.

WEATHER AND WHEN TO GO

Provençal summers are long, hot and dry, and temperatures reach their peak in July and August when the sea is warmest, the landscape is parched (with a serious risk of forest fire) and the Camargue is unbearably humid. From late September to November, storms bring sudden heavy downpours to revive the landscape. At this time, too, the vines are adorned with rich autumn hues.

Winters are mild, quite dry and sunny but with snow on the mountain tops (the lower Alps are usually cloaked in snow from November to early April).

Striking contrasts

WEATHER AND WHEN TO GO

Watching the world go by

Spring is a lovely season, bringing an explosion of wild flowers and clouds of almond blossom from March onwards. The worst feature of the weather is the vicious *mistral* (from the Provençal word for 'master'), a penetrating north wind that sweeps down the Rhône valley at any time between autumn and spring. Nobody should underestimate the stinging force of this cold wind which can make being out of doors most unpleasant. After the tempest, however, all is calm and clear.

July and especially August are best avoided – unless you specifically want to go to one of the festivals – because at this time of year Provence is overcrowded, overpriced, clogged with traffic, hot and bad-tempered. If you want hot weather without the seething hordes, choose early June or late September.

From March to May the weather is mostly sunny, the scenery looks bright and fresh, and you can appreciate the major historic sights in peace (some smaller sights may still be closed in March). October, too, can be warm, and though there is a risk of storms, they quickly clear. There is less going on in winter, when some hotels and sights may be closed, but you will enjoy tranquillity and better weather than in northern climes.

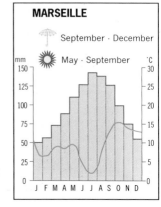

HOW TO BE A LOCAL

Provence was an independent nation for centuries and its people still have a fiercely independent spirit. They are deeply proud of their history, traditions and culture – which should be shown respect. Most Provençaux are friendly, generous, hospitable and helpful once you have broken through their initial reserve. It also shows respect to address people as *monsieur, madame* or *mademoiselle*. A smattering of French goes a long way to oiling the wheels of social encounters – it shows you are making an effort to appreciate their way of life.

In inland, rural areas, the locals are more conservative in their outlook than those in the cosmopolitan cities and coastal resorts who are more used to the unbecoming, even vulgar, behaviour of some visitors. On beaches, topless sunbathing is perfectly acceptable – in fact it is almost the norm – and there are designated areas for nude sunbathing. Walking around town in beachwear can cause offence, however, and you should show respect when visiting religious buildings. The Provençaux have diverse origins, but many have a hot-blooded Latin temperament – this can be seen in daily life (such as in cafés and restaurants) and on special occasions (like *fête* celebrations), when they are lively, zestful, demonstrative and given to lots of laughter. Likewise, any disagreement can quickly become very animated. Food and wine, the land with its crops and flowers, art and culture are all held dear to their spiritual hearts. And some of the local customs have much to recommend them – like truly relishing – even rhapsodising – over your meals, sitting in a café or on a bench in the main square gossiping and watching the world go by, promenading along the main street in the early evening, playing *boules*, shopping in markets and sampling the food before you buy, discussing politics and sport, putting your heart and soul into enjoying traditional events. By following such local examples, you can relax into the Provençal way of life, and make the most of your visit.

CHILDREN

Youngsters are genuinely welcome in restaurants, some of which offer special children's menus; if not, you can usually find dishes to suit their tastes, such as steak *hachis* (like a burger) or chicken and chips. Most hotels will supply extra beds if you want your children to share your room (for a small supplement), and a few have children's beds or cots available. There is often a discount on *demi-pension* for children, and in smaller, family-run hotels the owners may be willing to babysit if you go out. Campsites usually have lower rates for children, and a few have child-care facilities. Fares on public transport are lower for children and museums charge a reduced entrance fee (infants are generally admitted free). The following attractions are specifically aimed at younger visitors.

Aquacity Near Plan-de-Campagne, just north of Marseille, an 'aquatic jungle park' with pools, water-shoots, rapids and special shows. *Open:* June to early September.

Aqualand By St-Cyr-sur-Mer/Les Lecques, east of La Ciotat. Another aquatic park with many watery amusements. *Open:* June to mid-September.

Château de la Barben East of Salon-de-Provence, a castle and zoo with all sorts of exotic animals, plus train rides. *Open:* daily.

El Dorado City Just north of Carry-le–Rouet, and 8 miles (13km) west of Marseille, this Wild West town features various spectacles put on by stuntmen and actors, with train rides, a puppet theatre and playground. *Open:* daily June to mid-September; limited opening from mid-March to May and mid-September to mid-November.

OK Corral At the southern foot of the Massif de la Ste-Baume, 9 miles (14km) east of Aubagne, this is a Wild West funfair with lots of thrilling rides and spectacles. *Open:* daily, end April to early September; limited opening March, April, September and October.

Le Village des Automates Just east of St-Cannat, west of Aix, a theme park with colourful animated scenes and puppets. *Open:* daily April to September, limited opening October to March.

TIGHT BUDGET

● Go out of season, as prices are often lower. Hotels and most *gîtes*, for example, are up to 30 per cent cheaper in June and September, and even cheaper in the low season.

● Cheaper places to stay include one or two star *Logis* hotels, *gîtes d'étape*, campsites, and *Auberges de Jeunesse* (Youth Hostels). See also **Accommodation** and **Camping/Student and Youth Travel** in the **Directory** section).

● Avoid cafés situated on the main square, where you will pay for *cachet* as well as your drinks. A *bar-tabac*, tucked away in a back street, will be cheaper than a chic terraced café in a prime central location.

● The cheapest places to eat out are brasseries in towns and villages, or roadside restaurants displaying the Relais Routiers sign. Choose the simplest *menu fixé* (fixed-price) menu and look for special low-priced lunch menus.

● Shop at markets for the best value in food, crafts and cheap clothing such as T-shirts and sandals. Hypermarkets are good value for food and wine.

● Buy wine directly from the *vignerons, Coopératives* or *Maisons du Vin.*

● Take supplies of toiletries, film and medicaments, as these items are expensive to buy in Provence.

● Some municipal and national museums and monuments have free or reduced-rate entrance one day a week (often Sunday).

● Avoid *péage* motorways – the tolls can be quite an expense.
● Use a credit card to pay your bills as you will get a better rate of exchange. The same is not true, however, of cash advances, because you pay a high interest rate. Instead take your money in the form of traveller's or Eurocheques and shop around for the best rate.

SPECIAL EVENTS

Provence buzzes with special events of all kinds, especially in summer. The region's internationally renowned arts festivals are a magnet for culturally inclined visitors from many countries. The most celebrated is Avignon's **Festival of Dramatic Art**, held in July and August (see page 29), closely followed by Aix's

prestigious **Festival d'Art Lyrique et de Musique**, in July (see page 75). Traditional, local festivals and *fêtes* abound in the towns and villages of Provence. Many celebrate age-old rural events, such as the harvest, or important products, such as wine or lavender. Others have religious or folkloric roots, such as the colourful **gypsy** *pélerinage* (pilgrimage) in Les Stes-Maries (see page 66) and the **Tarasque festival** in Tarascon (see page 62). Local festivals are picturesque events, where you are likely to see locals in traditional costumes; they are also a good excuse for a knees-up, when the food and drink flow freely.

Cattle herders of the Camargue celebrate in Arles

SPECIAL EVENTS

Below are listed the main arts festivals and a few *fêtes*; there are hundreds more – ask at tourist offices for information.

May
Arles (1st), Fête des Gardians in honour of the cattle herders of the Camargue. **Les Stes-Maries** (24th and 25th), Pélerinage des Gitanes (Gypsy Pilgrimage). **St-Rémy** (Whitsun), Fête de la Transhumance, celebrating the ancient sheep migration from the plains to the mountain pastures. **Apt** (Whitsun), Cavalcade music festival.

June
Arles, Rock'Stival (rock festival). **Tarascon** (last weekend), Fête de la Tarasque, celebrating the defeat of a legendary monster. **Aix** (month end), En Musique arts festival.

July
Aix, Festival International d'Art Lyrique et de Musique, Festival International de Danse and Provençal week. **Arles**, Le Festival (of music, dance, opera and theatre), and Les Rencontres Internationales de la Photographie. **Avignon**, Festival Provençal and Festival d'Art Dramatique. **Carpentras**, Festival Passion (music, dance and theatre). **Fontaine-de-Vaucluse/L'Isle-sur-la-Sorgue**, Festival de la Sorgue (music, theatre and dance). **Gordes**,

Harbour scene, Les Saintes-Maries-de-la-Mer

festival of theatre, classical music and jazz. **Marseille**, Festival de Folklore de Château-Gombert, and Festival des Iles. **Orange**, Chorégies festival of opera and classical music. **St-Rémy**, Festival Organa of organ music plus jazz. **Salon**, Festival de Jazz. **Vaison-la-Romaine**, festival of music, theatre and dance.

August
Aix, Festival de Jazz. **Châteauneuf-du-Pape**, Fête de la Véraison. **St-Rémy** (15th), Charrette Fleurie. **Arles**, Festival du Film Peplum. **Entrecasteaux**, Festival International de Musique. **Séguret**, Festival Provençale. **Avignon** (end of month), *fête*.

September
Arles, Fête des Prémices du Riz, rice-harvest festival. **Cassis**, Fête des Vins Cassis.

October
Les Stes-Maries (Sunday nearest 22nd), Pélerinage de Stes Marie Jacobé et Marie Salomé (pilgrimage).

SPORT

Tourist offices in Provence have plenty of information on sports, but if you have special requirements you should contact the following national organisations.

Cycling There are marked cycle routes in some areas, and bikes are widely available for hire (ask at tourist offices). The Fédération Française de Cyclotourisme, 8 Rue Jean-Marie Jégo, 75013 Paris, has further information.

Golf Details from the Ligue de Golfe, Golf des Milles, 13100 Aix-en-Provence.

Hiking Very popular in the high, hilly areas of Ventoux, the Lubéron, Alpilles, Mont Ste-Victoire, the Massif de la Ste-Baume and the Massif des Maures. There is a good system of marked footpaths – *Sentiers de Grandes Randonnées*. For information contact the Fédération Française de la Randonnées Pédestres CNSGR, 8 Av Marceau, 75008 Paris.

Horse-riding There are *centres équestres*, *clubs hippiques* and ranches all over Provence. The Délégation Nationale au Tourisme Équestre, 170 Quai de Stalingrad, Parc de l'Ile St-Germain, 92130 Issy-les-Moulineaux, has lists of addresses.

Mountaineering Contact the Club Alpin Français, 12 Rue Fort Notre-Dame, 13007 Marseille.

Watersports For information on **sailing** and **windsurfing** contact the Comité Départemental de Voile et Planche à Voile, 13 Le Port de la Pointe Rouge, 13008 Marseille. For **waterskiing** contact the Fédération Française de Ski Nautique, 16 Rue Clément-Marot, 75008 Paris. For **canoeing** and **rafting** contact the Fédération Française de Canoë-Kayak, 87 Quai de la Marne, BP58, 94340 Joinville-le-Pont. For **fishing** contact the Conseil Supérieur de la Pêche, 134 Avenue de Malakoff, 75016 Paris. For **scuba-diving** contact the Fédération Française des Sports Sous-Marins, 24 Quai de Rive Neuve, 13007 Marseille.

Directory

This section (with the biscuit-coloured band) contains day-to-day information, including travel, health and documentation.

Contents

Arriving
Camping
Car Rental
Crime
Customs
  Regulations
Disabled Visitors
Driving
Electricity
Embassies and
  Consulates

Emergency
  Telephone
  Numbers
Health
Holidays
Lost Property
Media
Money Matters
Opening Times
Pharmacies
Places of Worship

Police
Post Office
Public Transport
Senior Citizens
Student and Youth
  Travel
Telephones
Time
Tipping
Toilets
Tourist Offices

Arriving

Entry Formalities

You only need a passport to enter France if you are a citizen of an EC country, the Council of Europe (except Turkey), the US, Canada, Japan, Australia and New Zealand; citizens of other countries need a visa as well, but check, before your visit, with the French Consulate to see if the situation has changed.

By Air

There are frequent direct scheduled flights to the region's two main international airports

Sun, sea and sand make Provence a watersports paradise

at Marseille and Nice. By booking at least two weeks in advance, you can take advantage of the cheaper Apex fares. There are also lower-priced charter flights – and last-minute bargain fares to be found – but to be sure of a flight in high season, it is best to book well in advance (when fares are more expensive). Marseille is more convenient than Nice for visiting west Provence; it is 105 miles (168km) by toll motorway from Nice to Aix. Alternatively, you could fly to Paris and take an internal flight or a train. Marseille-Provence airport is about 10 miles (16km) northwest of the city at Marignane, by the Etang de

Berre. Nice-Côte d'Azur airport is located some 4 miles (7km) southwest of the resort, by the sea.

Both these airports are small but efficient, with a range of facilities including *bureaux de change*, car rental desks and duty-free shops. Apart from taxis, there are regular bus services into the town centres and to railway stations nearby.

By Train

The French National Railways (SNCF) offers a very good service. To reach Provence by day you can take the TGV (*Train à Grande Vitesse*), which runs from Paris to Avignon in 3hrs 45mins, and to Marseille in 4hrs 40mins. If you are going to northeast Provence, you can take the TGV to Valence or Grenoble and change to an ordinary train. At night there are sleeper trains which, on average, take twice as long as the TGV.

Holders of a France Vacances pass (which is sold only outside France and allows you four days of unlimited travel within fifteen days or nine days within a month) can use the TGV but must pay a small seat reservation charge. The pass does not include accommodation on a sleeper. Pass-holders can also obtain discounts on Air France flights to Paris from many British airports, or on the Hoverspeed Channel crossings. The pass also offers discounts on car hire, some hotels and public transport in Paris.

You can take your car to Provence on SNCF's efficient motorail service, from

Boulogne, Calais or Dieppe to Avignon, Fréjus/St-Raphaël or Nice; or from Paris to the same destinations, plus Marseille, Toulon or Gap. Further information from overseas branches of the French Railways, which has branches in many capital cities (in the UK contact the French Railways, 179 Piccadilly, London W1V 0BA; tel: (071) 493 9731).

After the summer of 1993 the Channel Tunnel (via the TGV) will connect Paris with London in 3 hours.

By Coach

Numerous bus companies operate long-distance coach services to Provence from the major European capitals (eg from Brussels, Paris, Geneva and Barcelona). From London, National Express Eurolines run coaches to Marseille either direct or via Grenoble, a journey of 22 or 24 hours duration, (tel: (071) 730 0202 or (0582) 404511).

By Car

The fastest route to Provence from northern Europe is the Autoroute du Soleil (the A6 from Paris, which becomes the A7 after Lyon). The total distance from Paris to Marseille is 494 miles (790km). Toll charges add to the cost of the journey, but it is faster to stick to the motorway because most of the alternative roads take winding mountainous routes and are much slower than their distances look on the map. Even so, it can be more relaxing to drive down the N7, which takes a more westerly route south of Paris to Lyon (but

Relics of a gentler age; horse-drawn carts in a Provençal olive grove

is almost the same distance) and then runs parallel with the motorway. This may prove the better route at weekends in the skiing season, and throughout July and August when the *autoroute* is very congested and subject to long delays.

Camping

There are numerous campsites all over Provence and they are graded from one to four stars (with corresponding price levels) according to their facilities. The best have a restaurant, shops and swimming pool on site. Other options include *campings à la ferme* and *aires naturelles de camping*, usually small simple sites with few facilities. Lists can be obtained from branches of the French Government Tourist Office or local tourist offices (see page 124).

Car Rental

A car is essential if you want to explore the more rural parts of Provence, and there are plenty of places where you can hire a car for a couple of days or longer. The major drawback is the price: car hire is more expensive in France than in many other European countries. Airlines and tour operators offer fly-drive packages which are often more economical than hiring locally within Provence. Some inter-national car-hire companies offer discounts for booking in advance, or special deals which can make it cheaper to arrange rental in your home country than with the same company in France. Most companies have a minimum age limit of 21 or 23 and you must have held your licence for at least a year. To hire a car, you need to show your driving licence and credit card. Local tourist offices have lists of car hire companies in their area.

DIRECTORY

Sculpted by nature

Crime

Though Marseille is notorious for the activities of the *milieu* (the underworld) the city has, in fact, a lower crime rate than Paris and visitors are not likely to be affected. Petty theft is, however, a common hazard, especially on the coast and in the cities. You should take all the normal precautions: carry your purse safely, do not flash large amounts of money around, keep your camera and valuables secure (with you, or in a hotel safe), always lock your car and never leave anything valuable inside – cars, especially foreign vehicles, are popular prey for thieves. Make sure you have travel insurance covering such eventualities, and keep a separate record of cheque numbers, credit card numbers and emergency telephone numbers (such as for cancelling cheques). If you are an unlucky victim, report the incident to the local *gendarmerie* – make sure they give you a record of your statement for your insurance claim. If you have any problems, contact your nearest consulate (see page 117).

Customs Regulations

The allowance on items that EC visitors may take into France or take back to their own countries, without paying duty, varies according to whether the goods were bought tax-paid in ordinary shops and other outlets, or in duty-free shops. The allowances are as follows (the lower amounts for items on which duty has not been paid is shown in brackets):
300 (200) cigarettes, *or* 150 (100) cigarillos, *or* 75 (50) cigars, *or* 400g (250g) of

tobacco; 5 litres (2 litres) of still table wine, plus 1.5 litres (1 litre) of alcohol over 22% vol/38.8° proof, *or* 3 litres (2 litres) not over 22% vol/38.8° proof or fortified sparkling wine; 75g (50g) of perfume and 375cl (250cl) of toilet water; 1kg of coffee, *or* 200g of tea, *or* 400g of instant coffee or tea, *or* 80g of essence. Nobody under 17 years is allowed to take alcohol or tobacco.

You may also bring back goods up to a value of 2,800F (700F for visitors under 15 years) without paying duty – including 2kg of fruit or vegetables (except potatoes), five plants or parts of plants (not chrysanthemums or trees), a small bunch of cut flowers, and 50 litres of beer.

NB: New and generous duty-free allowances are due to be introduced shortly, but these will only affect goods purchased and exported within the member countries of the EC.

Disabled Visitors

Wheelchair-bound visitors will need help to negotiate the steep, cobbled streets of many Provençal towns. Hotels can present a problem too, because they are often in old buildings, with steep steps and stairs and narrow doorways. Hotels (and campsites) suitable for disabled visitors are indicated in tourist office lists – but it is essential to check whether they suit your requirements before you go, as the interpretation of 'disabled facilities' varies widely. Disabled parking badges are recognised in France, but it still may be difficult to find free parking space near major sights and monuments. Branches of the French Government Tourist Office abroad have an information sheet for disabled visitors, and main tourist offices within France also have free booklets with useful local information. The following organisations have published holiday guides for the disabled: RADAR (Royal Association for Disability and Rehabilitation), 25 Mortimer St, London W1N 8AB (tel: (071) 637 5400 – they also have an information department that can give advice); CNFLRH (Comité National Français de Liaison pour la Réadaptation des Handicapés), 38 Boulevard Raspail, 75007 Paris; Association des Paralysés de France, 22 Rue Gérard, 75013 Paris.

Driving

A car is often the only way of exploring the dramatic Provençal countryside, and especially for reaching remote villages.

Documents

The minimum age for driving is 18. You need a full driving licence (an international licence is not required for visitors from Western Europe, the US, Canada, Australia or New Zealand), the vehicle's registration document and an insurance certificate. A green card is no longer compulsory, but it is advisable as it provides fully comprehensive cover.

In addition, you must display a disc at the rear of the vehicle identifying the country of origin (eg GB).

DIRECTORY

Speed Limits

Unless otherwise signposted, the limits are as follows (lower limits, given in brackets, apply in adverse weather, such as when the roads are wet, icy or fogbound): 130kph/80mph (110kph/68mph) on toll motorways; 110kph/68mph (100kph/62mph) on dual carriageways and non-toll motorways; 90kph/55mph (80kph/50mph) on other roads. In towns a maximum speed limit of 50kph/31mph applies from the point where you encounter the name sign, to the exit sign (where the name has a bar through it); there are often sleeping policemen (speed bumps) on the roads entering towns and villages, to make sure you slow down. *Rappel* road signs mean a continuation of the restriction or of the previously signposted speed limit.

Rules of the Road

Keep to the right. In built-up areas, you must give way to cars coming from roads to the right as they have priority; it is vital to be vigilant as this includes even the most minor side-turnings. Traffic on main roads outside built-up areas usually has the right of way at junctions and crossroads – these are signposted with a cross saying *Passage Protégé*, by a thick arrow crossed by a thin line, or by a yellow diamond on a white background. A yellow diamond crossed out means you do not have the right of way. The priority-to-the-right rule no longer applies at roundabouts,

where you must stop and give way to cars already on the roundabout – as indicated by a sign with arrows running in an anticlockwise circle, saying *Vous n'avez pas la priorité*. You must also give way at any sign which says *Cedez le passage*. On entering a town, follow the signs saying *Centre Ville* to reach the historic core, where you can usually find the tourist office. When leaving a town follow the signs saying *Toutes Directions* until you see a sign for the place you want to go. Within towns, streets marked *Sauf Riverains* are forbidden to all but the cars of residents.

Parking

This is a major problem, especially during the day, and the police are very strict – ignore signs indicating that illegally parked cars will be towed away at your peril. Short-term street parking is available in clearly signposted *Zone Bleue* areas; you must buy a ticket from a nearby machine and display it in the car. There are also large car parks with automatic barriers and ticket machines – take the ticket with you, insert it into the machine on your return and pay the specified amount; the ticket will be returned so that you can insert it at the exit barrier.

Petrol

There are plenty of petrol stations along main roads, with many open in the early evening; motorways have 24-hour service stations. Those on more minor roads are likely to be closed on Sunday. There are far fewer petrol stations in remote mountainous areas, so do not get caught short. Unleaded petrol is widely available. Maps showing petrol stations are available from main tourist offices.

Breakdowns
A red warning triangle must be carried if your car does not have hazard warning lights – it is advisable to carry one anyway, in case the breakdown affects your lights. The triangle should be placed 100 feet (30m) behind the car. Motorways have emergency phones every 1.25 miles (2km); otherwise contact the police for advice on local emergency services.

Accidents
Take down the number of the other car and exchange insurance details with the other driver. Try to take the names and addresses of any witnesses, then contact the police to make a statement.

Driving Violations
The police can charge on-the-spot fines for drink-driving, speeding, not wearing a seatbelt, parking violations and so on.

Electricity
Generally the supply is 220 volts using round two-pin plugs; adaptors are needed for non-Continental appliances. Some remote areas may still have a supply of 110 volts.

Embassies and Consulates
Australia: 4 Rue Jean-Rey, 75724 Paris, Cedex 15 (tel: (1) 40 59 33 00).
Canada: 35 Avenue Montaigne, 75008 Paris (tel: (1) 47 23 01 01).
Ireland: 12 Avenue Foch, 75116 Paris (tel: (1) 45 00 20 87).

Festive flags in Arles

DIRECTORY

New Zealand: 7 Rue Léonard-da-Vinci, 75016 Paris (tel: (1) 45 00 24 11).
UK: 35 Rue du Faubourg St-Honoré, 75383 Paris Cedex 08, and its consular section at 9 Avenue Hoche, 75008 Paris (tel: (1) 42 66 38 10); 24 Avenue du Prado, 13006 Marseille (tel: 91 53 43 32).
US: 2 Avenue Gabriel, 75382 Paris, Cedex 08 (tel: (1) 42 96 12 02/42 61 80 75); 12 Boulevard Paul-Peytral, 13286 Marseille (tel: 91 54 92 00).

Emergency Telephone Numbers
Police: 17
Fire: 18
Ambulance: 15
SOS Doctor: 91 52 91 52 (Marseille); 90 82 65 00 (Avignon); 42 26 24 00 (Aix)
SOS Dentist: 91 25 77 77

Provençal stoneware

Health
No vaccinations are required for visiting Provence. EC citizens should obtain form E111 (from post offices) before departure to be eligible for free treatment or reduced medical costs. It is quite safe to drink the tap water served in hotels and restaurants; but never drink from a tap labelled *eau non potable*.

Holidays – Public and Religious
New Year's Day
Easter Sunday
Easter Monday
Labour Day (1 May)
VE Day (8 May)
Ascension Day
Whit Sunday and Monday
Bastille Day (14 July)
Assumption Day (15 August)
All Saints' Day (1 November)
Armistice Day (11 November)
Christmas Day

Lost Property

Report loss of valuables to the police and obtain a copy of the statement for making an insurance claim. Cancel lost credit cards and traveller's cheques immediately. A lost passport should be reported at once to your nearest embassy or consulate, which will also issue emergency documents.

Media

Le Monde is the most serious and respected French national daily newspaper. Two regional newspapers are useful for information on local events and entertainment: *Le Provençal* (which leans to the left) and *Le Méridional* (very right-wing). Large town newsagents also sell a selection of foreign newspapers – usually a day or so late – and magazines.

Money Matters

The French franc (denoted as F or ff) is divided into 100 centimes. There are notes of 20F, 50F, 100F and 500F in circulation, and coins of 5, 10, 20 and 50 centimes, 1F, 2F, 5F, 10F and 20F.
Foreign currency, traveller's cheques and Eurocheques can all be changed at banks, and some cards can be used in bank cash machines. Bank opening hours vary, but are typically Monday to Friday 09.00–12.00hrs and 14.00–16.00hrs. All banks are closed on Sunday and public holidays. Some are open on Saturday but closed on Monday. Bureaux de Change often stay open later, and are only closed on Sunday. Post offices will change Giro Bank

Postcheques and Eurocheques. You can also change money in some hotels, and in main tourist offices. Rates of exchange and commission vary widely enough for it to make quite a difference if you are changing a large amount of money, so it is best to shop around.
Carte Bleue (Visa/Barclaycard), Eurocard (Mastercard/Access), American Express and Diners Club are widely accepted in hotels, restaurants, petrol stations and classier shops; many places also accept Eurocheques.

Opening Times

Almost everywhere closes for a couple of hours at lunchtime, although main museums and tourist offices stay open all day in the high season and you can usually find a petrol station open. Normal business hours are 08.00 or 09.00–12.00hrs and 14.00–18.00hrs.

Shops

Hours vary, but they typically open 09.00–12.00hrs and 14.00 or 15.00–19.00 or19.30hrs. Small food shops, including *boulangeries* (bakers) often open as early as 07.30 or 08.00hrs. Food shops and supermarkets close at 12.00hrs and often do not reopen until 15.00hrs or later. Shops may open later in summer than in winter, sometimes until 20.00hrs or later. Most shops are shut on Sunday, and many shut all day Monday as well. You can usually find a bakery open every morning, including Sunday. Most markets operate in the mornings only; some take place on Sunday.

DIRECTORY

Museums

Monuments and museums typically open 09.00 or 10.00–12.00hrs and 14.00–18.00hrs. Hours are often shorter in winter, and longer in summer when some major sights remain open over the lunchtime period. All are closed on Christmas Day and New Year's Day, and usually on public and religious holidays. Many close one day a week, some in the low season only. Typical closing days are Monday (for municipal museums) and Tuesday (for national museums and historic monuments), but this can vary. Smaller sights may close altogether in winter. Churches and cathedrals are usually open all day except during services. If you want to see a church that is locked it is worth asking at a nearby shop or at the priest's house, the *presbytère*, to see if you can obtain a key.

Pharmacies

Pharmacies – recognised by their green cross sign – provide a wide range of medical advice. There is always one open in the area by rota, all night and on Sundays and public holidays (*pharmacie de garde*) – details are posted on pharmacy doors.

Places of Worship

Catholic churches are found in every town and village. Ask tourist offices about other local churches. There are synagogues in Avignon, Carpentras and Cavaillon.

Police

In cities and towns, police duties are carried out by the *Police Municipale* (wearing blue uniforms). The countryside and smaller places are covered by the national police force of *Gendarmes* (blue trousers, black jackets and white belts). Emergencies and riots are dealt with by the CRS – *Compagnies Républicaines de Sécurité* – who also look after safety on public beaches. The highway police are the *Garde Mobile* or *Police de la Route*.

Post Office

The PTT (*Poste et Télécommunications* or *Bureau de Poste*) deals with mail and telephone services. Main post offices are usually open 08.00 or 8.30–19.00hrs on weekdays, 08.00–12.00hrs on Saturdays; smaller offices usually open shorter hours and may close for lunch. All sell stamps and phone cards, while some will change cheques (see **Money Matters**, above). Stamps and phone cards are also sold in *tabacs* (tobacconist shops, often found in cafés). Letter boxes are yellow.

Poste Restante

You can arrange for letters to be sent to you Poste Restante at main post offices, for a small fee; letters should be addressed to you, Poste Restante, Poste Centrale, with the town postcode and name. Each *département* in France has a postal code – and each town has its own number which begins with the first two digits of the *département* number. Thus the code for towns in Bouches-du-Rhône is 13000; Vaucluse is 84000; Var is 83000; and Alpes-de-Haute-Provence is 04000.

Public Transport

Air
The French internal airline, Air Inter, links many domestic airports – including Avignon, Marseille and Toulon, in Provence (information from Air France or travel agents).

Inspiring landscapes

Bus
Services are punctual and comfortable, but not very frequent outside the main urban areas (rural buses tend to operate early in the morning to

Billowing lavender

suit school and market hours).
Even in cities, bus services
mostly stop by about 21.00hrs.
As buses are run by many
different private companies,
services are often not co-
ordinated. There are also SNCF
buses (run by the national
railways) – on which rail tickets
and passes can be used –
serving various places on rail
routes where trains do not stop.
Most sizable towns have a bus
station (*gare routière*), often
near the railway station – but it
is not necessarily used by all
the bus companies. Ask at the
ticket office or local tourist
office for help and advice.
(Gares routières, tel: Marseille
91 08 16 40, Aix 42 27 17 91,
Avignon 90 82 07 35.) The
SNCF also runs coach
excursions (information from
tourist offices or tel: 91 47 22
32).

Rail
Trains are fast, frequent,
reliable and comfortable. A
main railway line links the
towns and cities in the Rhône
valley, connecting with
Marseille and Aix, then running
east along the coast; another
main route runs along the
Durance valley, and continues
north to the Alps. Information
from tourist offices or stations
(tel: Marseille or Aix 91 08 50
50, Avignon 90 82 50 50). A

number of different discount tickets and passes are available, including the France Vacances pass (see page 112).

Senior Citizens

Senior citizens are eligible for reduced or free entrance to sights (aged over 60), and fare discounts on public transport (aged over 65).

Student and Youth Travel

For information on official French Youth Hostels contact the Fédération Unie des Auberges de Jeunesse, 27 Rue Pajol, 75018 Paris (tel: (1) 46 07 00 01); tourist offices can also help. In some large towns, *Foyers des Jeunes Travailleurs* are hostels providing comfortable, low-priced accommodation for students and young workers.

There are discounts for students on public transport, and reduced fares on trains for those aged under 26. Entrance charges for sights are usually lower for under-18s, or free at national museums with reductions for 18 to 25-year-olds.

A special youth card (the *Carte Jeune*), which is available to anyone under 26, entitles holders to discounts on public transport, museum admissions, entertainments, shopping and other facilities (including meals in university canteens); ask at tourist offices or post offices for details.

Telephones

To call anywhere in France just dial the eight-digit number – there are no additional area codes to worry about. Paris is an exception. To dial a Paris number from the provinces, you must dial 161 before the eight-figure number; if phoning from Paris to the provinces, dial 16 first; within Paris, just dial the eight-figure number.

Cheap rates apply on weekdays between 22.30 and 08.00hrs, from 14.00hrs on Saturday, and all day Sunday. When phoning from abroad to the French provinces, the international code (010 from the UK) is followed by 33 (for France) and then the eight-figure number; to Paris, the international code is followed by 331. For calls out of France, dial 19 (wait for a new tone), then the national code (eg: 44 for the UK) and the number, omitting the initial 0 of the area code (eg: 71 or 81 for London). French phone boxes are coin or card-operated. Phonecards (*télécartes*) can be bought at post offices, tobacconists and newsagents. Calls can be received at phone boxes with a blue bell sign. Some post offices have metered booths, where the calls are connected by a clerk and you pay afterwards. Bars often have coin-operated phones.

For directory enquiries, tel: 12; operator, tel: 13; time, tel: 3699.

Time

France observes Central European Time, which is one hour ahead of Greenwich Mean Time from late September to late March, and two hours ahead for the rest of the year

Tipping

Service is usually included on restaurant and café bills, but a

DIRECTORY

small additional tip is customary. Hotel bills generally include service, though porters expect a small tip in the more upmarket hotels. Otherwise give tips, as you would at home, to taxi drivers, hairdressers and tour guides.

Toilets

Dames for women and *Messieurs* or *Hommes* for men. In hotels, restaurants and cafés these are generally modern and clean. Occasionally you will come across the old-fashioned type with footrests where you squat. Modern, self-cleansing, coin-operated public toilets are found in the streets of some towns and cities.

Tourist Offices

The French Government Tourist Offices worldwide have plenty of useful information to help plan a holiday in France.
Australia: BNP Building, 12 Castlereagh St, Sydney NSW 2000 (tel: (02) 231 5244).
Canada: 1981 Avenue McGill Collège, Suite 490, Montréal QUE H3A 2W9 (tel: (514) 288 4264); 30 Saint Patrick St, Suite 700, Toronto ONT M5T 3A3 (tel: (416) 593 6427).
Ireland: 35 Lower Abbey St, Dublin 1 (tel: (01) 703 4046).
UK: 178 Piccadilly, London W1V 0AL (tel: (071) 491 7622).
US: 610 Fifth Avenue, New York NY 10020 (tel: (212) 757 1125); also at 9454 Wilshire Boulevard, Beverly Hills, CA 90212 (tel: (213) 272 2661).
The following regional tourist delegations in France can

provide a lot of useful information, including details of all types of accommodation in their area.
Comité Régional de Tourisme:
Provence-Alpes-Côte d'Azur, 2 Rue Henri-Barbusse, 13241 Marseille Cedex 01 (tel: 91 39 38 00).
Comité Départemental de Tourisme:
Bouches-du-Rhône, 6 Rue du Jeune-Anacharsis, 13001 Marseille (tel: 91 54 92 66);
Vaucluse, Place Campana, La Balance BP147, 84008 Avignon (tel: 90 86 43 42);
Var, 1 Avenue Vauban, 83000 Toulon (tel: 94 09 00 69);
Alpes-de-Haute-Provence, 42 Boulevard Victor-Hugo BP 170, 04005 Digne (tel: 92 31 57 29).
In France, many towns and villages have an *Office de Tourisme*, or a *Syndicat d'Initiative*, which is smaller and may not open every day (especially in winter). Look out for the *i* (information) sign. They are generally very helpful, with lots of useful information on such things as accommodation and transport, what to see, entertainment and sports. Some change money, and a few will help book hotels for a small fee.
The following larger tourist offices are open all day during the summer, with shorter hours on Sunday, public holidays and in winter.
Aix-en-Provence: 2 Place Général-de-Gaulle, 13100 (tel: 42 26 02 93).
Arles: Esplanade des Lices, 13200 (tel: 90 96 29 35).
Avignon: 41 Cours Jean-Jaurès, 84000 (tel: 90 82 65 11).

LANGUAGE

English is spoken by those involved in tourist trades and in the larger cosmoplitan towns – less so in smaller, rural places. Your efforts to speak French will always be appreciated.

Basic Vocabulary

yes oui

no non

hello/good morning bonjour

good evening bonsoir

goodbye au revoir

please s'il vous plaît

thank you (very much) merci (beaucoup/bien)

sorry pardon/excusez-moi

do you speak English? parlez-vous anglais?

I do not understand je ne comprends pas

toilets les toilettes

no smoking défense de fumer

entrance entrée

exit sortie

breakfast le petit déjeuner

lunch le déjeuner

dinner le dîner

coffee/tea café/thé

the bill, please l'addition, s'il vous plaît

shops les magasins

open ouvert

closed fermé

market le marché

bakery la boulangerie

newsagents/stationers la librairie

library la bibliothèque

chemist la pharmacie

food shop l'alimentation

butcher la boucherie

delicatessen la charcuterie

fishmongers la poissonerie

I would like... je voudrais

how much...? combien...?

where is...? ou se trouve...?

one un/une

two deux

three trois

four quatre

five cinq

six six

seven sept

eight huit

nine neuf

ten dix

eleven onze

twelve douze

twenty vingt

fifty cinquante

one hundred cent

one thousand mille

Monday lundi

Tuesday mardi

Wednesday mercredi

Thursday jeudi

Friday vendredi

Saturday samedi

Sunday dimanche

INDEX

INDEX
Page numbers in *italics* refer to pictures

accommodation 101–2, 123
see also individual towns for details
Aigues-Mortes 67
airports and air services 111–12, 121
Aix-en-Provence 6, *14*, 68–75, *69*, *75*
Allemagne-en-Provence 84
Les Alyscamps (Arles) 50
Ansouis 37–8
Apt 38
Aqueduct de Roquefavour 68
Ardèche Valley 93–4
Arènes (Arles) 50, *52*
Arles *11*, 49–56, *52*, *54*, *56*, *107*
Atelier Paul Cézanne (Aix-en-Provence) 70
Aubagne 68
Aups 82
Avignon 21–9, *22*, *25*, *27*, *29*

banks 119
Banon 86
Barbentane 57
Barjols 82
Barrage de Bimont 72
Le Barroux 45–6
Les Baux-de-Provence *57*, 57–8, *91*
Beaucaire 62
Beaumes-de-Venise 47
Bonnieux 38–9, *39*
Boulbon 49
Brantes 45, *45*
budget tips 106–7
Buisson 48
Buoux 39, 91
buses 121–2

Cabriès 72
calanques 10, 77
Camargue 10, *64*, 64–7, 87–9, *89*, *107*
camping 102, 113
car rental 113–14
Carpentras 31
Cassis 77,77
Cathédrale Notre-Dame-des-Doms (Avignon) 23
Cathédrale St-Sauveur (Aix-en-Provence) 70–1
Cavaillon 32
Centre d'Art Van Gogh 61
Centre d'Information de Ginès 65
Centre d'Information de Reserve Nationale 65
Chaîne des Alpilles 10, 49, 91
Chartreuse du Val de Bénédiction 35
Château d'Avignon 65
Château de la Barben 80
Château d'If 78
Château du Roi René 62
Château de Sauvan 85–6
Châteaudouble 82
Châteauneuf-du-Pape *19*, 32
children 105–6
La Ciotat 77
climate 103–4
coach services 112
Comtat Venaissin 9, 20, 34
Corniche Sublime 82, 84
Cotignac 81, *81*
credit cards 119
Crestet 48
crime 114
La Croix de Provence 72
culture, entertainment and nightlife 102
see also individual towns for details

currency 119
customs regulations 114–15

Dauphin 86
Dentelles de Montmirail 10, 45
disabled visitors 115
driving in Provence 115–17
driving to Provence 112–13

East and Central Bouches-du-Rhône 68–80
eating out 95
see also individual towns for details
Eglise St-Trophime (Arles) 50–1
embassies and consulates 117–18
emergency telephone numbers 118
En Vau 77
Entrecasteaux 81–2
entry formalities 111
Etang de Vaccarès 65, 88–9
Eyguières 80

Faucon 48
festivals and events 107–9
Fondation Vasarely 71
Fontaine-de-Vaucluse 42, *42*
Fontvieille 58, 60
food and drink 95–100
Forcalquier 84, *86*
Fort de Boux 39, 91
Fox-Amphoux 82

Gigondas 46
Golfe de Fos 10
Gordes 15, *43*, 43–4
Gorges de la Nesque 11, 45, 46
Grand Canyon du Verdon *4*, 11, 82, *83*, 84, 93
La Grande Crau 9, 49, 90–1
Grasse 100

Grottes de Calès 80
Grottes de Thouzon 33

L'Harmas 34
health matters 118
history 13–17
L'Isle-sur-la-Sorgue 32–3

Jouques 72

Lac de Ste-Croix 84
Lacoste 39–40
Lafare 47
landscape 9–13
language 125
local etiquette 105
local time 123
lost property 119
Lourmarin 40–1
Lubéron 37–41
Lurs 86

Maillane 61
maps
 Aix-en-Provence 70
 Arles 51
 Avignon 26–7
 Bouches-du-Rhône 54–5
 France 6
 Marseille 78
 Provence 20–1
 Var and Alpes 85
 Vaucluse 28
maquis 94
Marseille 6, 77–9, 79
Massif des Cèdres 41
Massif de la St-Baume 10, 68
media 119
Méjanes 65
Ménerbes 40, 41
money 119
Monieux 46
Mont Ventoux 10, 45, 94
Montagne du Lubéron 10
Montagne Ste-Victoire 8, 10, 68, 72
La Montagnette 49
Montmajour, Abbaye de 60

Moulin de Alphonse Daudet 58
Moulin Vallis Clausa 42
Mourre Nègre 37
Moustiers-Ste-Marie 84
Musée Arbaud (Aix-en-Provence) 71
Musée des Aromes et du Parfum 100
Musée Calvet (Avignon) 23
Musée Camarguais (Camargue) 65
Musée d'Art Chrétien (Arles) 51
Musée de Cire/Agricole (Camargue) 65
Musée Granet (Aix-en-Provence) 71
Musée d'Histoire Naturelle (Aix-en-Provence) 71
Musée Lapidaire d'Art Païen (Arles) 52
Musée Louis Vouland (Avignon) 23
Musée du Petit Palais (Avignon) 23
Musée Pétrarque (Fontaine-de-Vaucluse) 42
Musée Réattu (Arles) 52
Musée des Tapisseries (Aix-en-Provence) 71
Musée Theodore Aubanel (Avignon) 23
Musée Tsigane (Camargue) 66
Musée du Vieil Aix (Aix-en-Provence) 71–2
Museon Arlaten (Arles) 52–3
Museon Frédéric Mistral (St-Rémy-de-Provence) 61

Nîmes 13, 36
North Vaucluse 45–8

Notre-Dame-de-Salagon 84–5
Observatoire-de-Haute-Provence 86
opening times 119–20
Oppède-le-Vieux 41
Orange 10, 30, 34, 35

Palais des Papes (Avignon) 5–6, 23–4, 25
La Palissade 66
Parc Naturel Régional du Lubéron 37, 91–2
Parc Ornithologique 66
Pavillon Vendôme (Aix-en-Provence) 72
La Petite Crau 9, 49
pharmacies 120
Pic des Mouches 72
places of worship 120
Plateau d'Entremont 72
Plateau de Vaucluse 41–4
police 120
Pont du Gard 36, 36
Pont Julien 38
Pont St-Bénézet (Avignon) 21, 24, 29
post offices 120
Provence Orchidées 57
public and religious holidays 118
public transport 121–3

rail services 112, 122–3
Rasteau 47
Reillanne 86
Rhône 9
Riez 84
Rocher du Cire 46
La Roque Alric 47
Roussillon 44
Routes des Crêtes 84

St-Gilles 67
St-Hilaire, Abbaye 40
St-Michel-de-Frigolet, Abbaye 63
St-Paul-de-Mausole 61

INDEX

St-Rémy-de-Provence 59, 60, 61–2, 100
Stes-Maries (Les Saintes-Maries-de-la-Mer) 66–7, 67, 108
Salon-de-Provence 79–80
Sault 46
Séguret 46–7
self-catering 102
Sénanque, Abbaye de 44
senior citizens 123
Sérignan 34
shopping 100, 119
Silvacane, Abbaye de 80
Simiane-la-Rotonde 86
Southwest Haute-Provence 84–6
sport 109

student and youth travel 123
Suzette 47

Tarascon 49, 62–3, 63
telephones 123
Théâtre Antique (Arles) 53
Théâtre Antique (Orange) 34
Thermes de Constantin (Arles) 53
Le Tholonet 72
Le Thor 33
Thoronet, Abbaye du 82
tipping 123–4
toilets 124
tourist offices 124
Tourtour 82
travelling to Provence 111–13

Trigance 16, 84
Uzès 36

Vacqueyras 47
Vaison-la-Romaine 12, 47, 47–8, 48
Var and Alpes-de-Hautes-Provence 81–6
Vaucluse 20
Vauvenargues 72
Venasque 34–5
Village des Bories 39, 43
Villecroze 82
Villeneuve-lès-Avignon 35–6
voltage 117

West Bouches-du-Rhône 49–63
West Vaucluse 20–36
wildlife 87–94

Acknowledgements

The Automobile Association wishes to thank the following photographers and libraries for their assistance in the preparation of this book.

RICK STRANGE took all the pictures in this book (© AA PHOTO LIBRARY), except:

NATURE PHOTOGRAPHERS LTD 92 Salvia (B Burbidge), 94 Greater Flamingos (L H Brown)

PICTURES COLOUR LIBRARY LTD cover Vaucluse

SPECTRUM COLOUR LIBRARY 56 Pont de Langlois Arles, 59 St Rémy, 60 Les Antiques, St Rémy, 76 Cassis, 79 Old Port Marseilles, 80 Fish, 97 Flan, 98 Kitchen, 107 Festival Arles, 110 Windsurfing

A WILSON 45 Brantes Ventoux

The publishers would also like to thank the following for their assistance:
Holiday Autos, 12 Bruton St, London W1X 7AJ (tel:071-491 1111)